American Freestyle Karate: A Guide to Sparring

by Dan Anderson

DEDICATION

This book is dedicated to my first class of private students (January, 1977). Without their trust and faith, this book would never have come about: Heather Stadick, Neal Stadick, Denise Winn, Mike Bakkum, R. S. Sevryn Wright. Also to my first partner, Janesa Kruse, my first black belt, Randy Thomas, and to my long time student, friend and partner through thick and thin, Bill Rooklidge.

Without all of you, my development and one of its products, this book, would only have been a dream.

ACKNOWLEDGEMENTS

The creation of this book is due to the influence and support over the years of a great many people. To list everybody would require a full section of this book, so I am thanking in print some of the principles and the rest of you, we both know who you are.

My instructors: Loren Christensen (1966–1967); Mike Engeln (1966–1969); Bruce Terrill (1966–1974); My teammates in the Wu Ying Mun black belt class during a crucial stage of my early development (1971–1974); and Steve Armstrong, Don Williams, Bob Barrow in the Pacific Northwest.

Bill Wallace, Howard Jackson, Jeff Smith, Demetrius Havanis, Roy Kurban, John Natividad, Darnell Garcia, Benny Urquidez, Steve Sanders and the entire BKF crew, Al Dascasos, and Mike Anderson in my early national tournament days (1970–1975). I would like to acknowledge special thanks to Bill Wallace who, prior to the publication of this book, went over the basics of his special kicking method, corrected me where it was needed, and okayed this presentation in this book.

My current top ten peer group: Keith Vitali, Bobby Tucker, Ray McCallum, Jimmy Tabares, Larry Kelley, John Longstreet, Harold Burrage, Mike Genova, George Chung, Karen Shepard, Belinda Davis, Tayari Casel.

A special tip of the hat goes to Chip Wright of Medford, Oregon; Fred King and Tom Levak of Portland, Oregon; Steve Fisher of Los Angeles, California; Jack Farr of Enid, Oklahoma; Mike and Sheila Dillard and the entire Century crew of Oklahoma City, Oklahoma for their special friendship at special times.

Thanks go out to Dean Sutera and Larry Kennedy, my job supervisors, for their indulgence. About 90% of this book was written at work.

To Kathy Weckel for expert typing and patience beyond the call of duty. She put up with my last-second changes, extreme impatience and mood changes better than any crack team of combat psychologists could have.

Thanks to Ed Ikuta for the photography of the text, to Heather Stadick, Mary Townsley, Maggie Townsley, for some of the action photos, the Unique Publications staff for their aid in preparation of this manual, and to Bill Rooklidge, my partner in the photos.

Also, special thanks go out to Renardo Barden and Leslie Kerr for their initial interest and encouragement in this work and to Paul Maslak who got after me to finish it. Thanks to LRH for his inadvertent aid and instruction.

DISCLAIMER

Please note that the publisher of this instructional book is NOT RESPONSIBLE in any manner whatsoever for any injury which may occur by reading and/or following the instructions herein.

It is essential that before following any of the activities, physical or otherwise, herein described, the reader or readers should first consult his or her physician for advice on whether or not the reader or readers should embark on the physical activity described herein. Since the physical activities described herein may be too sophisticated in nature, it is *essential that a physician be consulted.*

UP UNIQUE PUBLICATIONS

7011 SUNSET BLVD., HOLLYWOOD, CALIF. 90028-7597

©UNIQUE PUBLICATIONS INC., 1982

Printed in the United States of America
ISBN: 0-86568-021-3
Library of Congress No.: 81-50512

TABLE OF CONTENTS

FORWARD

This book is one I searched for as a 14-year-old white belt back in 1966. My own instructor was teaching me the basics of karate, but I hungered for a book that could show me all sorts of "fancy moves" and "tricks" in sparring.

The type of books on the market then and today are 1) beginning primers, 2) self-defense, 3) weapons primers, 4) style specialties, 5) other martial arts (Judo, Tai Chi Chuan), and 6) history books. There have been several books that cover certain techniques for sparring that have been written recently, but they fail to satisfy my original needs. Robert W. Smith, a fairly well known author on various Chinese martial arts, once wrote in a review of a martial arts book, "Give me the principles and I'll devise my own tactics."

That is what I was looking for. Give me the idea and I'll see how it works for me and under what circumstances. That is what this book is all about. What is covered here is what is covered in my classes and, in fact, is an expanded version of a packet of printed reference material that I hand out to my students.

So, go over the material and see what interests you and what directly relates to your own sparring. When you find something that does, study it until you have the idea or concept down pat.

AMERICAN FREESTYLE KARATE IN PERSPECTIVE

I started karate in November 1966 in Vancouver, Washington, under the instruction of Loren Christensen and Mike Engeln. The style of karate we practiced was Kong Su, a pre-unification Korean method that resembled Shotokan karate. At the time I began, Kong Su was being modified with some Wing Chun Gung Fu ideas by our organization's head instructor. I trained with Loren and Mike through brown belt level and then began direct instruction under Bruce Terrill, receiving my first-degree black belt in January, 1970, and my second-degree black belt in January, 1973.

It was then that I began my main drive in competition, and my competitive endeavors helped me to expand my own growth in karate. Within three years of my promotion to black belt, I was being rated in the Top Ten National competitors periodic ratings and have for the last three seasons ('77–'78, '78–'79, '79–'80) been rated in the yearly top ten by the *Karate Illustrated* ratings system and also have been rated in the top ten by the STAR Ratings system by *Inside Kung-Fu* Magazine. My overall record shows 60 Grand Championships including several Western States titles, a Martial Arts Ratings Systems Grand Championship, a Mid-American Nationals Grand Championship, plus being the anchor man on the first-place team in the 1974 International Karate Championships.

In the summer of 1974, I began to work on devising my own training methods for a group of private students, breaking away from the Wu Ying Mun style (the style Kong Su evolved into). Using my previously gained knowledge and continuing to compete on the national circuit, I picked up a healthy amount of input which helped me in devising my own method of instruction. In 1979, I and a black belt student of mine, Janesa Kruse, set up our first school, and later in mid-1980, we expanded our base of instruction into two schools. I was also promoted to third-degree black belt by the American Karate Association in May of that year.

"American Freestyle" is the name tag I give to my method of instruction in order to convey the idea of a non-oriental type of karate. Rather than the idea of a set style to be passed on from master to senior student, I liken my studio and method of karate to that of a boxing gym headed by a particular trainer (e.g. Muhammad Ali's camp headed by Angelo Dundee or Floyd Patterson's camp headed by Cus D'Amato). Not exactly the traditional way karate is looked at, but then again, this is not a very traditional style.

This concept in karate instruction and, I feel, any style of American Karate, owes tremendous debts to Bruce Lee, Chuck Norris, Joe Lewis and Mike Stone. In 1967, Bruce Lee came out in print and denounced non-progressive, traditional methods of Gung Fu and flatly advised any practitioner to experiment rather than blindly follow anything that was told to them. This, coming from an Oriental, especially one as skilled as Lee, was taken as a godsend by every martial artist who wanted to expand and experiment but did not because of peer group pressure. Slightly earlier or about the same time on the tournament circuit, Chuck Norris started revising his fighting style to aid his winning in tournaments. He began adding punching methods and moving combinations to the previously kicking-oriented Tang Soo Do training and became a much more rounded fighter. Joe Lewis expanded on training given him by Bruce Lee to revolutionize karate beyond the mechanical technique level to an operational approach level that helped karate's progression jump about ten years forward in a space of a few years. As early as 1963, Mike Stone introduced Western-based positive mental attitude training besides the physical training to replace Oriental attitude training to Americanize his style.

Overall, the Dan Anderson method of American Freestyle Karate acknowledges these martial artists and Muhammad Ali, from whose style and artistry I have borrowed liberally.

MECHANICAL APPROACH

In almost every karate book, a large portion of the book is devoted to the mechanics of karate. The mechanics of any style of karate, gung fu and tae kwon do are basically the same. They all kick, punch and block. The differences in the mechanics are usually in slight degrees; for example, using a "standing fist" (thumb up) for a straight punch rather than a "flat fist" (thumb down), etc. The basic approaches to the techniques are the same from style to style—a straight punch goes straight, a round kick goes round and a downward block goes downward. There are only so many ways to move the body, regardless of what the moves are called or the degree of significance attached to them.

I have found that the main differences in styles are based on 1) cultural/historical background, 2) style emphasis points (kicking over punching, attack over defense, etc.), 3) instructor preferences within his own school and 4) kata (forms) idiosyncracies.

The ideas and approaches in this book can be used by anyone from any style or method and, therefore, whatever basics you have been taught can be used to implement them. That is why I am not illustrating hundreds of pages on punches, kicks, blocks and stances as in a basic karate primer. The mechanics I do illustrate are included because 1) they may not be executed in the manner of the accepted norm, 2) they may not be in common use or 3) they are used for the explanations in Part 2 of this book. Therefore, you won't see spearhands, knife hand blocks or jump spin axe kicks. I have included only what I actually use, or may use in explaining the offensive and defensive approaches or uncommon but effective techniques.

STANCE AND POSTURE

Front

The basic front stance is between an extended position and a natural stand. The front stance is similar to a boxer's foot position and is used for its mobility.

a) *Feet Position:* One shoulder-width forward and back. The lead foot should be turned slightly inward so that in conjunction with the way you are facing, the little toe is in line with the inside of your heel. The rear foot is positioned so that the heel/toe alignment is facing straight toward your opponent as is your lead foot. The rear heel is up off the floor and both knees are bent. Imagine that the front knee is on the corner of a box that is exactly your shoulder width square. If your feet go off the corners, you fall off the box.

Rather than standing straight up in this foot position, you should get the feel of "sitting" in the stance. Your weight is evenly distributed on both feet with the rear heel up. Keep from leaning over the front foot, thereby putting more weight on the front foot.

Your hips and shoulders should angle away from the direction of the rear foot, thereby placing your whole body at a 45 degree angle position to your opponent. Your head and neck face straight forward.

Avoid two gross errors: Getting the feet one in front of the other in a line (thin or shallow stance). If your feet are aligned, your sideways balance is almost non-existant. Also avoid getting your feet too wide in a stance; you are asking to get kicked in the groin.

b) *Hand Position:* Bring your fists up to shoulder height and rest your elbows at the side of your ribs. Rest your rear fist on the same side breast but don't "stick" it there tightly. Put your lead fist in front of the same side breast at one fist's width distance from the body. Point both fists at the opponent rather than at the ceiling. Keep the knuckles aimed at your opponent's nose.

Remember to keep both elbows well bent. Do not let the lead arm drift out from the body like an antenna or let the rear arm lower its position. Your lead hand is always the same as the lead leg forward!

Side

The basic side stance is merely a sideways variation of the front middle stance. It is used for mobility but also has potential for implementing side facing kicks.

a) *Feet Position:* Your feet are a shoulder-width apart facing at a 90 degree angle from the direction your head is facing. The feet are parallel to each other with the rear heel raised. The knees are well bent. Your hips and torso should be totally sideways to your opponent with your head turned so that it is facing him. Looking at your stance in a mirror, you should only be able to see your lead shoulder.

b) *Hand Position:* Your lead fist should be as high as your shoulder and aligned between your opponent and under your nose. Your rear hand will rest on the opposite side breast, lightly touching but not "sticking" to it. Both fists point directly at your opponent.

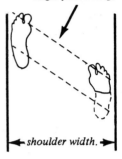

Hip and shoulder angle positioning.

shoulder width.

Front stance.

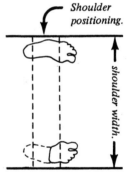

Shoulder positioning.

shoulder width.

Side stance.

Horse Stance

This stance is used as a change-of-pace stance shifting from a "high riding" posture to a "low sitting" one. It is also a great position to create the illusion of increased distance between you and your opponent. It as not as mobile as either the front stance or side stance.

    a) *Feet Position:* Your feet are two shoulder-widths apart and as parallel as possible. Push your knees outward and create the impression of sitting. Your butt should be tucked under and your back straight. Your basic side stance hand position applies here also.

    b) *Alternative Hand Positions:* There are two basic alternative hand positions I teach; they are basically "guard" positions. They are the high guard and low guard, based on the positioning of the lead hand. Rather than being in an en-garde/ready-to-hit position, these positions are shields covering certain areas.

        High Guard—The lead biceps/upper arm area is resting against the ribs. The lead fist is resting about the distance of a fist and a half in front of the lead breast. The rear arm's biceps rests alongside the ribs and the hand covers the front of the groin. The angle of the body is facing to the side, but not quite fully sideways. A side stance or horse stance is the foot position.

        Low Guard—The lead arm biceps rests against the lead side ribs and the hand covers the front of the groin. The rear biceps and elbow rests on the ribs just a few inches to the side of the solar plexus, and the lower arm (fore arm, fist) is held verticle so that the fist is near the jawline. Again, a side-facing stance is most suitable for this guard.

        As you can see, these guards place the arms in a position to shield any vital area from attack with a minimum of body movement. Their main drawback is that only certain types of attacks can come from these guards with a minimum of telegraphing; for example, it is going to be difficult to disguise a lead hand downward hammer fist from the low guard position, but a lead back fist from the same position comes quite naturally.

The stances I have listed have many variations and a fair-sized book could be written just listing all the different stances people use. These are the ones that I find useful.

The basic hands-up position is good for attack and is excellent for blocking. The guards are good for certain attacks and excellent for shielding your body if you are uncertain about your blocking or just have a preference for shielding.

BODY MOVEMENT WITH FOOTWORK

Body movement is categorized into two parts: a) footwork and b) body movement excluding footwork. I will outline and give explanations for the various types of footwork and body movements used in American Freestyle Karate as their uses will be further explained in the Offensive/Defensive approach section of the book.

Footwork is one of the most important mechanical aspects of karate. If you can't move

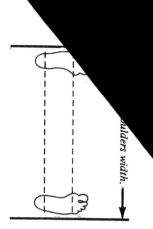

Horse stance.

High guard.

Low guard.

...nation, you won't hit your opponent or keep from being hit. It is

...otwork has evolved from the early Frankenstein monster stiff-
...f quick bursts, easy gliding and coordinated grace. We all owe
...e for telling us Americans that it is okay to be innovative in
...lly, but that is exactly what happened) and Muhammad Ali
...scene when he did. There is not a top American karate
...ited at least one aspect of the Ali footwork repertoire.
...ork is broken down into three categories: 1) mobility, 2) entry and 3) retreat.

Mobility

This is used when you are setting up or feeling out your opponent. You are simply keeping a mobile base. At white belt level, a constant circular walk in one direction or the other is sufficient. As you become more coordinated, different types of bouncing and circling are added. You can cross step, simple front or side bounce. With the cross step and bounce, you want to set up an easy rhythm; a relaxed movement that does not tax you. You can remain relatively in one position or circle around your opponent as you move.

The basic idea is to not "sit" on your opponent. It is too easy to be sucker shot when you plant yourself in one position or sit dead on somebody. Also, your take-off action in your attack is going to be that much more telegraphed if you start from a standstill. Then, there is also *inertia* to consider.

Webster's New Collegiate Dictionary's definition of inertia is "a property of matter by which it remains at rest or in uniform motion in the same straight line unless acted upon by some external force." It applies to footwork when you want to change non-motion to motion or motion to non-motion. The external force in changing non-motion to motion is the leg muscles. Have you ever wondered why your initial move does not explode, especially from a standstill? It's because of the inertia (non-motion) that must be overcome (changed to motion). From a standstill, your leg muscles have to tense up and begin working into the leg action desired to bridge the gap. This initial starting is going to be slower than the final speed reached because the leg muscles are starting from a dead stop. A car does the same thing; builds up speed from a stop ("0 to 60 mph in 6 seconds" TV commercial. Why not 0 to 60 *right now?* Because of the weight of the car, the wheels are not turning, etc. Inertia). Inertia is very important to overcome. If you are moving, the leg muscles are already in action, so all you have to do is accelerate the muscle action at the time you desire to make the initial move explosive. You are accelerating moving weight instead of moving dead weight. Then, if your initial move is still sluggish, you can trace it to not enough commitment and poor timing.

Now, on to mobility.

a) *Circular Walking:* I start beginners on circular walking since they have been walking all their life. Here, you merely walk the periphery of your opponent's critical distance line. I prefer that you walk to your own "front," forward stepping rather than backward stepping, although you can walk backwards. When circle walking you want to keep your lead fist, shoulder, hip and head pointed at your opponent at all times. This way you will be in position for an adequate attack or defense.

1   *Right step.*

4   *Rotate to left*

2   *Rotate to left.*

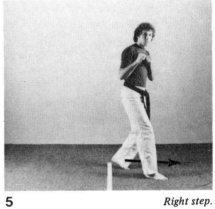

5   *Right step.*

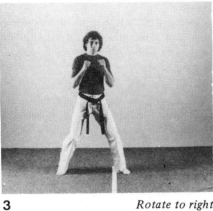

3   *Rotate to right*

6   *Original stance.*

Circular walking.

Walk normally with emphasis on keeping your knees bent and your head level but don't formalize this action so that it starts being unnatural. Also, don't try to sneak around, like a spy in the movies; just walk. The main thing to watch for is getting out of alignment with your opponent.

Work on being able to go in one direction and then change to the opposite direction. Use the step of the rear leg to pivot off to twist and change direction with. Don't drift through the transition; that is a great place to get hit.

b) *Stationary Bounce:* This is just bouncing up and down. The idea here is to get the feel of constant movement, an easy rhythm that does not tax you. You want to flex at the knees and ankles, not just the ankles. In the beginning, if you bounce just off the ankles you will get a quick hop but not an easy bounce. At this stage you want to develop a flow of motion so that you can work on coordinating your actions easily. When you can do that, then we can get into breaking up the rhythm. First develop the flow of motion so that you are not doing a series of singular bounces, but one giant action consisting of bouncing. Make sure you bounce on the balls of your feet and not on the flats. A lunge comes especially easily from this movement.

c) *Forward-Back (bounce):* My own nickname for this is the "rope skip" as it approximates a step used in skipping rope and differentiates it from the stationary bounce.

How do you do it? From your stance, step forward on your lead foot about six inches, set it down, bring your rear foot forward the same distance, set it down. Then, take the rear foot back six inches, set it down, and then the lead foot back the same, set it down. Forward—back, forward—back. That's it. Do the step until you get a continuous rhythmic feel for it and then do it with a bounce. The bounce is deceptively harder than the step but still fairly easy to learn.

This type of motion is easy to use for creeping up on your opponent or to set up a false lead (broken rhythm). Do not cover much distance with each single step; this is not an entry method but a mobility step. Use it to creep and move but not for gap bridging.

To circle with this step, instead of bringing the rear foot forward, pull it slightly behind you so that with each bounce you will be rotating toward your rear using your lead foot as your axis point. For circling toward your front, instead of bringing your rear foot straight back to the original position (the beginning of the step back portion of the step), take it diagonally to your front. Then pull the lead foot back in alignment with your opponent. As you do this consecutively, you will circle toward your front.

I know it is hard to work with photos, but when looking at the footwork photos, do it first in sets of twos; 1-2, 3-4, 1-2, 3-4. Like morse code rhythm; dot-dot, dash-dash. When that is coordinated, then 1-2-3-4, 1-2-3-4, 1-2-3-4. After that, do it in sets of 5, 7, 10, and then continuously. First stepping and then bouncing. If you get frustrated, go over the "Gradient Learning" section of this book and then go over the illustrations again. It will come with practice and patience.

d) *Cross Step (bounce):* This is also a bounce pattern and is basically a side facing pattern. A cross step is a stationary bounce but scissoring the legs as you bounce. The trick here is to not cross your legs very far nor let them go outwards very far, but to make a short easy motion. An easy way to get the feel of how far to scissor

9

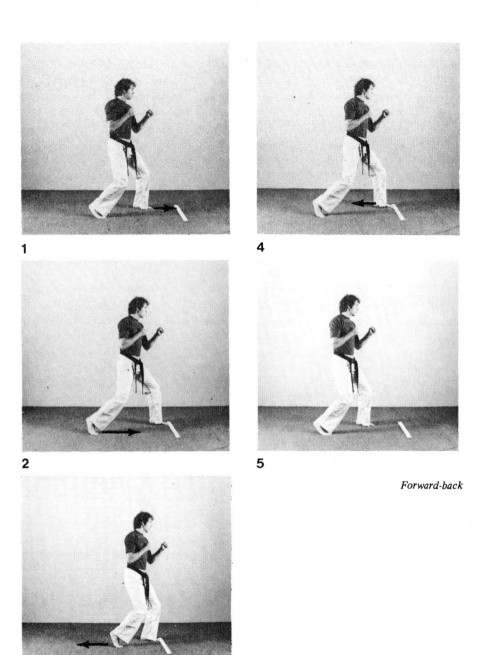

1

2

3

4

5

Forward-back

your legs and then return them to an outward position is to draw a straight line and align it with you facing your opponent. On the scissor motion, both feet just cross over the line, on the return they again just cross over the line. There is a tendency to dramatize the action and scissor too much, setting yourself up as an easy target.

After a while, you will get a feel for the correct distance. There is also a tendency to sit a split instant prior to the next bounce—don't, unless you are breaking the rhythm on purpose. Otherwise, keep the movement continuous. Avoid springing up and down and don't let your head bob more than a few inches, otherwise you will be just "trampolining" and that won't help your ability to move.

To turn, let your rear leg (on the scissor action) cross behind farther than on the stationary cross step and use both legs to slightly turn to your rear so that you will face at an angle to your original direction. To move in a circle, do the same as turning but when you go outward from the scissor action, step out with your lead leg a bit farther than on the bounce so that with the further stepping of the rear leg (on the scissor action) and lead leg (coming out of the scissor action), both feet will be stepping toward your rear. Get the idea of following your rear leg and it will come easier.

A note on circular moving: Keep the idea of following your rear leg and use the lead foot as a pivotal point. You need not keep the lead foot stationary (actually, in most cases you should not), but keep it aligned with your opponent. On circling toward your front, do somewhat of a shuffle/skip motion, leading with your rear leg. Here you break out of the cross step bounce to do the circle to the inside, but go back into it when the circling is complete. Do not extend on your sideways step with your rear leg since that will really open up your groin area. When circling to the rear, do not go out of alignment with your opponent and turn your back even slightly on him; you will be asking for trouble.

Entry

Entry is getting from point A, outside of range, to point B, where you can hit your opponent effectively. This is actually bridging the gap between you and your opponent. A lunge, slide up, skip, spin or run-step would be used here. A lunge, skip and run-step must be explosive, like a bullet shot from a gun. You can regulate the timing of a slide up and spin on either full speed or less than full speed.

Entry is the idea of "you gotta get there." Where? To your opponent. How? Here is how.

a) *The Lunge:* From "front stance," the foot position of the basic fighting stance, push off the rear foot. As you do, extend the lead leg as far as you can, pointing the toes ahead of you. This extension step should cover at least one shoulder-length distance. As the lead foot sets down, use the tightening of the leg muscles so that the lead leg brakes the forward progress of the body. This way, you keep from falling over your lead leg. As you brake, the lead knee is behind the foot but in line with the shin and ankle. As your foot brakes the body action, your rear foot slides up to a stance position twice as fast as the lead leg extension. It is pulled by the forward motion of the rear knee.

Moving the feet only about a shoulder length or so forward is a preparation to the lunge called the "easy step." When you feel comfortable with the easy step, increase the distance so that rather than being able to step across the distance, the rear leg has to propel the body across. This is a bit more difficult. The push-off pressure of the rear foot should be directed downward and back so that your body

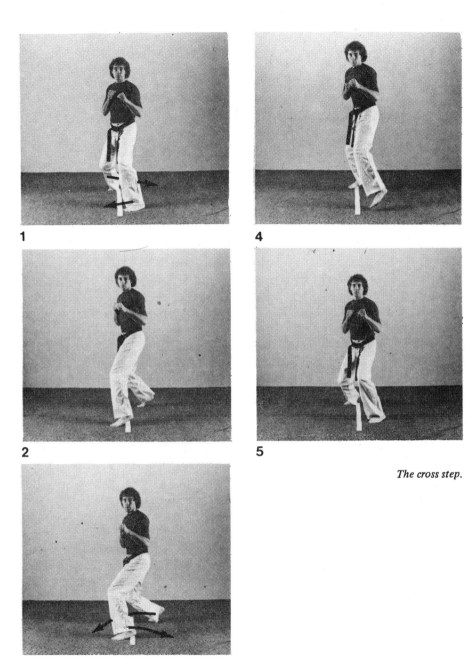

1

2

3

4

5

The cross step.

will be propelled forward only. A common mistake is to push your body upward rather than forward. The head and shoulders should move in a straight line and not bob up and down when lunging.

Of paramount importance is the quickness of the takeoff. Quickness is the suddenness with which you take off rather than the miles per hour speed/velocity you

The lunge.

3

attain. The quickness of the lunge is likened to a bullet coming out of the chamber. When the gun is fired, the bullet does not straighten its back, see if its stance is okay, brace its back leg, etc. It goes—NOW! When you lunge, so do you. This is a move which requires lots of practice and time to master.

When you lunge at your opponent, you need to have full commitment in your action and nothing less; otherwise it will greatly impede your chances of successfully bridging the gap. Also, refer to the section on "Reach" in this book as a conceptual aid in lunging.

Watch for common errors: (1) Rocking or resting your weight on the back leg before taking off. (2) Returning your rear foot too close to the lead foot. (3) Returning your rear foot to a shallow stance and being too sideways. (4) Dragging the rear leg stiffly back to a stance rather than lightly and quickly. (5) Not using the bend and flex of the knees to move.

On a lead leg lunge kick, pick up your lead leg a fraction of a second prior to the push off of the rear leg. Fire the kick *as* you are pushing off so that you minimize the time lag in the delivery of the kick. If throwing a side facing kick, make sure you are facing the side to begin with, as the additional body movement used in turning sideways from a front facing position will add to the time lag between

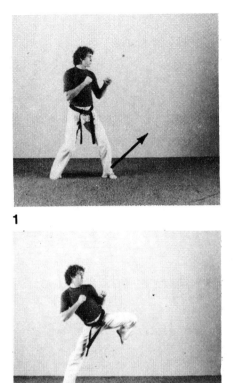

1

2

3

4

The lunge kick.

1

2

3

4

The rear leg-lunge kick.

1

3

2

4

The skip-side kick.

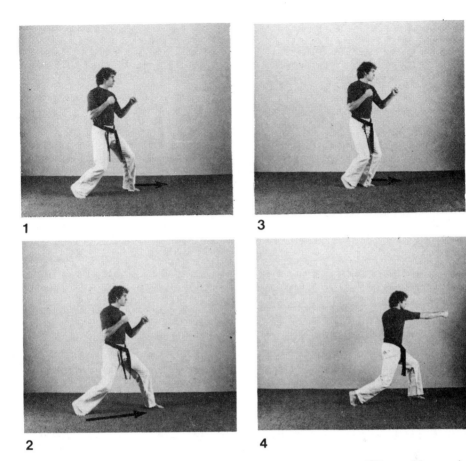

1

2

3

4

Slide up with a punch.

initial takeoff and hitting with the kick.

Watch out for three common errors: (1) Picking up the leg *and then* pushing off. (2) Unnecessary over-cocking of the leg. (3) Doing a simultaneous pickup and push-off *and then* kicking. All three cause a delay or time lag in your action to lunge kick your opponent. This approach is especially speedy if you take off from a mobile base (moving fighting position) and also if your opponent lets you in his range.

Something to keep in mind is that you want to go straight at your opponent. The lunge is easy to goof up by moving up rather than straight. A method of training for a correct lunge is what I call "Up and Under." Have your partner place his arm in front of you across your path at about forehead height. You bounce up once (to simulate a mobile base) and as you come down and land, push off on your rear foot forward and pass under the arm. If you go up at all, you will get smacked by your partner's arm as you pass. If you go straight, you will pass underneath. This should give you the feel for pushing off correctly. Then do a two-bounce, three-bounce up to a constant movement. You can also do this with the lead lunge kick.

16

b) *Rear Leg Lunge Kick:* This is an action which is more of a power drive action rather than an initial speed one. Here you use the pick-up and throwing forward of the rear leg to pull your body forward to cover distance. The rear leg lunge kick is the classic example of commitment in a kick. Use this type of kick for a follow-up action on an opponent who runs from you or is a leaner. However, it is not recommended against someone who is quick.

c) *Skip:* A skip is a light, quick action for kicking when right on the periphery of the critical distance line or just slightly inside. The object of this movement is that of displacing your lead foot with your rear foot so that you can kick with the lead foot. You are not trying to move a large body of mass (your body) across a distance, but merely displacing one foot with the other and keeping the body movement down to a minimum.

From a side or front position, the foot action is the same. Your rear foot steps (not slides) up to the lead foot. As it sets to the floor, the lead foot picks up and kicks. The lead foot picks up as the rear foot sets down, not after it touches the floor and plants for balance. The feet pass each other in mid air, one going up, the other going down. If the skip kick is timed right, your kick should make contact as your other foot plants solidly on the floor. When done lightly, this is an extremely fast movement, but it is limited by range.

When skip kicking and with any other footwork method of kicking, be sure to plant the support foot in whatever pivot position it needs to be in for the kick. If you set down and then have to do your pivot action for the kick, that causes a time lag between the decision to kick and finally hitting your target.

d) *Slide Up:* This is a longer, more flowing motion than the lunge or skip. The basic action is nearly the same as the skip. (1) You take a short step with the lead foot, about nine inches forward and then (2) bring the rear foot directly beside the lead foot, heel up and on the ball of the foot and then (3) extend the lead leg forward and slightly outward into your stance. You extend outward with your lead foot so that you do not end up in a shallow stance. The timing of doing a hand attack is to begin as the lead leg extends into the final stance.

A slide up kick is the same as a slide up punch, except at the end of (2) your foot plants flat on the floor and (3) your lead leg kicks and sets forward in a front stance. In the slide up motion, your head maintains an even position as you move across the floor. Your gap-bridging speed is not as fast as the lunge, but you have time to spot any counter attacks your opponent may throw while you move. Note: On kicks where your body position is to be sideways when you kick (i.e., round kick, side kick, etc.) you use the initial step to *position your body* for the kick rather than wait until your leg is up and then shift.

Footwork is used for setting your body up to deliver an attack, getting close enough and positioning your body. Then your attack hits. So do all of your preliminaries *prior* to the hit: body positioning, angles, pivots, the works.

The feeling you should have doing a slide up is one of an ocean wave moving up the shore, a steady, constant forward flow of motion, rather than the bullet out of the gun barrel explosion. This step is best used with combination attacks and fake setups.

17

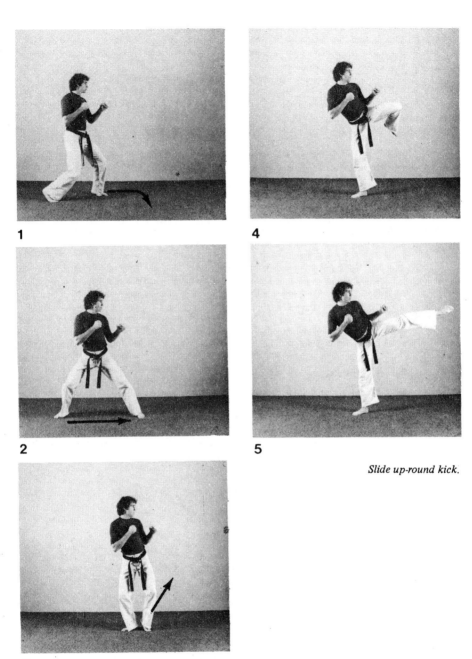

1

2

3

4

5

Slide up-round kick.

A note on footwork at this point. Do not put any weight on the moving foot during any footwork maneuver that involves sliding across the floor. Any weight on the moving foot will cause friction or unwanted drag and slow down the overall motion.

1

2

3

4

Slide up-front kick.

1

2

3

4

Spin-back kick.

1

3

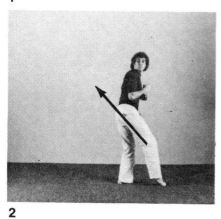

2

4

Spin-side kick.

1

3

2

Spin-round kick.

4

5

1

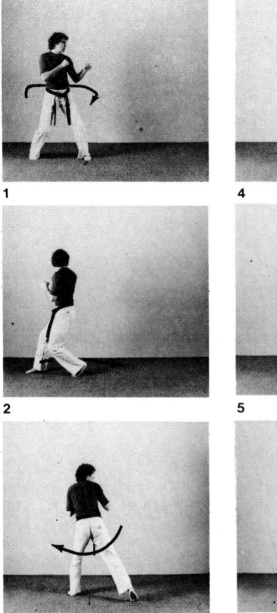

2

3

4

5

6

The 360 degree spin-round kick.

1

4

2

5

Spin-punch.

3

1

2　　　　　　　　　　**3**

Spin-back fist.

e) *Run Step:* As the skip is used primarily with your initial move being a kick, this is used primarily with a punch. This step was made popular by Chuck Norris back in the mid and late 1960s and later by Howard Jackson in the early 1970s:

The initial motion here is the lunge, but instead of ending it with a single lunge, you follow up with a full sprint at your opponent. This is the foot work most commonly used for a "blitz," a rapid fire, forward attack on your opponent. The blitz will be covered more at length in the "Attack by Combination" section.

This particular approach needs full commitment if it is going to work, especially on the initial move. Coordinate this from a moving action so that you will telegraph it as little as possible. Get the idea that the first move has to score and the follow-up is merely a backup. Do not get into the lazy attitude of "Oh well, if my first move doesn't get them, my follow-ups will." That is a classic example of mental and physical laziness with a good dose of non-commitment thrown in. The first move makes the others work.

f) *Spin:* Looking at it from a theoretical standpoint, doing a half or full turn to approach your opponent is downright risky, if not slightly suicidal, but you would be surprised how many people still get caught with an initial move spin back kick and even more so with a spin back fist or spin straight punch. Since I have nailed enough people on it, I will include it. A spin entry is used for a change up on your opponent and surprise.

Spin on the lead foot pushing off on the ball of the rear foot, twisting as you push. Your head must lead the body. You will find that if you get the head cranked around, the body will naturally follow. Closely watch an ice skater doing a spin in a routine. His head always turns before the body. In fact, it turns, stops and waits for the body spin to catch up, turns again, stops, etc. This is the same idea as the spin kick or spin punch. The head goes first so that you will whip your body around. Otherwise, you are just turning, not spinning. A spin is much faster than a turn. When spinning, spin on the ball of the foot and not the entire flat. If you are doing a spin kick, drop the spinning foot to a flat-on-the-floor position and brake your spin when you hit the exact preparatory position for the kick you are doing. Your preparatory position for the back kick will obviously be different than for the side kick or round kick. If you are doing a spinning back fist or punch, you will find that the spin is usually enough to off-set your opponent since a spin will generally precede a kick. Continue the spin into either a side facing position (for back fist) or front position (for straight punch). If you continue into a straight punch attack, set the "up" leg forward and go into a run step or stationary stance, depending on whether your opponent is standing or moving away.

Do not use the spin very often, but become proficient with it. It comes in handy at times.

Straight Rhythm—Broken Rhythm

Most foot work techniques are done in a straight rhythm. You start coming at your opponent at usually one speed and don't stop until you get there. You can feel the beat or pulse of your movement. Skip: pop-pop, Slide up: swish-swish-swish-swish, 1, 2, 3, 4. Conceptualize this, your entry is the dash (—) in Morse Code. Skip (——), slide up (————), lunge (—), your committed entry being the long dash. An uncommited step or false lead is the Morse Code dot (-). False lead—skip (-——), double false lead—lunge (--—), false lead in mid slide up (———-—), and so on. What happens to your opponent if he is expecting only committed actions from you? Most karate players expect that when someone comes at them that they are going to totally commit themselves at that instant. You can drive a person literally crazy with an extended series of false leads interspersed with committed actions. Most people cannot handle it. "Either come at me, damn it, or don't!"

If you get the idea of stuttering through a sentence and apply it to foot work, you've got it. A stutterer is not faking it. He is really trying to say a sentence. Your broken rhythm steps should not look like fakes, just breaks at the last instant. Once coordinated, broken rhythm is incredible. Broken rhythm is usually used in conjunction with arm, leg and body fakes.

Broken Rhythm—Mechanical Application

You want to apply broken rhythm to your entry to either upset or work off of your opponent's natural reaction or determined response. Directionally, your opponent has three options to your moving forward: He moves forward, he holds still, he moves away. Here, you are going to be working off of the response pattern rather than his technique counter. Keep in mind this one note: If you catch him off guard, what he will do is his natural response. His natural response may be flinch, jump up, a hit or whatever. This is what you want to work off of because the more confused your opponent becomes, the more "on automatic" he will get and the more on automatic he gets, the more he will do the same thing over again. Patterns will emerge that you will be able to work off of.

a) *Forward Response:* Your opponent comes at you to hit you as you move. The idea is to play the "I dare you to cross over this line" game that most kids play. There is a certain distance that you will have to cover in order to get your opponent to move at you, but in order to reach that distance you won't need the amount of commitment

1

4

2

5

3

6

Broken rhythm versus forward response.

1 **3**

2 **4**

Broken rhythm versus opponent holding a position.

necessary to fully cross the range to hit him. You do a half lunge, barely touch over that line and spring backwards to your original position and something interesting will happen. Your opponent, moving forward to your moving forward, will be used to only doing about a half a lunge's worth of distance covering (as he is meeting you about half-way across the range). When you spring backwards, his counter move will be out of range. The tricks here are to not plant yourself when doing the forward-back movement so that you can see two distinct, unconnected moves and to cover enough distance to make it look as if you are doing a fully committed action rather than just a half action. You can use this to either drive him into an extreme case of impatience so he will take off at you blindly so you can pick him off or to set him up into believing that you have got a case of hesitation during entry and then—bang—the real thing hits him. Just to be safe, this method is good to see just how your opponent will react and exactly what you want to use to set him up.

b) *Hold His Position:* This is where your opponent is going to plant and blast you on the way in. This type of response is when your opponent is going to react on your full commitment and generally has a decent eye for spotting commitment, so here is where we put it to use against him. Mechanically, what you are doing here is one-half of the action used against a forward response. You do a half lunge forward but you plant for a moment's hesitation, and then spring. What happens is that your opponent sees you coming, he begins his counter move (block, hit, etc.), it registers that you did not complete the commitment (your instant's pause), and he checks his counter move, you hit him during the check. Your half lunge has gotten you close enough so that you have very little distance to cover when you do close in and hit, but not so close that he can hit you on your move in. Here again the distance you cover is going to be crucial, close enough but not too close.

c) *Evasion Response:* This is the tough one. Your opponent here either is somewhat jumpy or is not about to be suckered. What you can do to this type of defensive response is to come forward in a series of short, stacatto-like bursts, until he gets in a defensive flow of motion and then blitz him (a blitz is covered in the Attack by Combination section). The tricks here are, do not come in with a series of rhythmically connected (same speed) steps because a good defensive fighter will, while backing up, match your forward rhythm and speed and then pop you one, and watch out for being set up by a fighter who will back up once, twice and then, bang, you get tagged as you move. Working against this particular type of response you have to be really alert. Is he jumpy or is he smart? Keep your eyes open.

Once you get your broken rhythm down so that it feels comfortable, intersperse it with straight rhythmic attacks so that your opponent will not know what you are going to do.

Line and Angle Fighting

As long as we are going over foot work entry, let's look at foot work approaches to sparring. There are line fighting and angle fighting.

a) *Line Fighting* is where you assume a straight forward and back approach to fighting your opponent. You move straight forward at him and straight away from him.

b) *Angle Fighting* is using an angular directional step to approach your opponent. On the offensive, at times you will take a preparatory step in order to angle in to your opponent or you might angle step past your opponent, hitting him as you pass.

In line and angle fighting, we are concerned with the entry and retreat aspects of foot work. You can either circle or stationary bounce or even stand still as far as preparation goes.

Most karate fighting is done in a line fighting approach; forward and back are the only directions that are used. While directness is a valuable asset to any fighter's approach, deceptiveness is just as valuable. This is where angle fighting comes into play. Angular stepping is especially useful when fighting an aggressive fighter who is stronger than you so that you can bypass meeting his strength head on. Also, you can use angular stepping to confuse your opponent prior to the actual attack.

When you and your opponent are fighting, you are connected by a line between you, much as though you held a rope taut between you. When you circle, the line moves as you move.

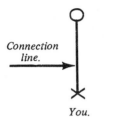

Connection line.

You.

Step and angle in.

Line Fighting.

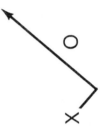

Step and angle past.

Angle past and hit.

1

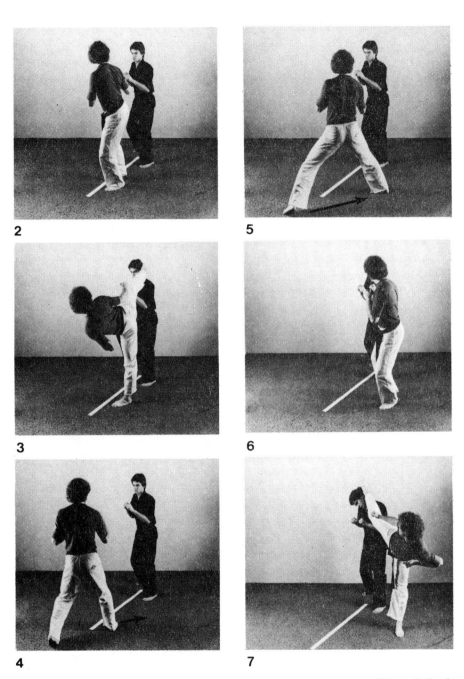

2

5

3

6

4

7

Angle past and hit with slide up-round kick to the head.

1

1

2

2

3

3

Angle past and hit-lunge punch.   *Angle step to intercept a circling opponent.*

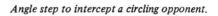

1

2

3

4

5

6

Angling to intercept a circling opponent.

The idea behind angle stepping is to first establish the connecting line between you and your opponent and then move off the line or cross it when you attack. Since most people fight in a line fighting manner, the connection is usually established from the beginning.

Your opponent will face you in a certain posture and that will establish the connecting line. When you angle toward his backside or front, generally he will shift to reestablish the line to its original posture. As he shifts, you angle in to him or past him and hit. This is what I will mean by crossing the line.

If your opponent is stationary, it is easiest to offset him by doing a preparatory step followed by an angle step to attack him or just to shoot a fast step past him and hit as you pass. If he is circling, you can angle in the direction of his circle and intercept him by shooting just slightly ahead of him.

An interesting thing about the connecting line; it is much like an elastic band stretched tightly from you to your opponent. It will extend to about a foot or so beyond your (or his) maximum range of extension. Beyond that, there is a feeling of disconnection, so keep that in mind if things are not going your way in sparring. Disconnect and then reconnect up again to start taking the initiative. If you want to drive an opponent crazy, disconnect every time he telegraphs an attack and then reconnect. After several of these, attack when he telegraphs. You will get him so he won't know if he's coming or going.

Here are the basic approaches to angular stepping:

1. *Angle past and hit.* This is one of the easiest methods of offensive angular attack as you shoot off of the connecting line just enough to get out of the line of his possible counter and still make it as compact an action as possible. The thing you want to watch out for is making the angle too wide and putting yourself out of range for your own attack. One very nice side effect of the angle past and hit approach is that it gives your attack a slightly different trajectory than if you were coming in on a straight line.

Example: Slide up round kick to the head. If you take a line approach you will hit the side of the head. On an angular approach, your body will be in a different position in relation to a line step and the trajectory of your kick will take it to the back of his head. If your opponent has a habit pattern of just guarding the side of his head, he will get smacked with the kick.

Utilize this idea with any technique you want and you will find a generality among karate players: They are most comfortable defending against an attack that travels along the connecting line. An attack that goes off the connecting line is out of sync with the blocking circuit (habit pattern) that they have set up for themselves; therefore, they have more problems handling that attack. You can set this up with a broken rhythm movement or do it direct. If your opponent is circling on you, you can angle step and intercept him.

2. *Step and angle in.* This is used in conjunction with doing a constantly changing footwork pattern. Circle left three steps, shift stance, false step, circle right two steps, retreat one half step, step forward, circle, step off and angle in—bang! You attack! The idea here is to use this move with other patterns of movement so that

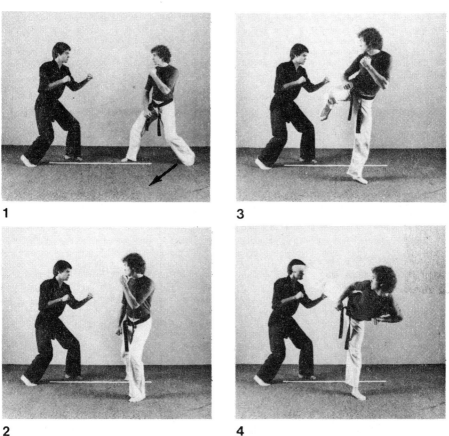

1

2

3

4

Step and angle within-side kick.

when you decide to step and angle in it will blend in with your other movements and not be so telegraphed. To do it without preliminary footwork, you might as well send them a telegram letting them know of your arrival time.

Basically, the idea here is to drive your opponent crazy with footwork and then hit him at an odd angle. Your preliminary step, if at all possible, should be some sort of a forward step so that when you spring on your opponent you won't have much ground to cover.

3. *Step in and angle past.* This is a combination of 1. and 2. If your opponent is keeping a tight watch on you as you set him up, throw a wrench into his works by angling past and hitting after the step. If he is keeping that tight a watch on you, then he is prepared for something that is coming *at* him, so do not come exactly *at* him.

This coverage here of line and angle fighting is just the offensive portion of it as it follows the entry portion of footwork. The defensive options will be outlined in the retreat section of Footwork and Evade and the Hit/Evade section of "Defensive Approaches."

34

1

2

Step in and angle past-straight punch.

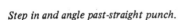

3

Retreat

The concept of retreat includes both retreating away from your opponent's attack and recovering from your own offensive move. Here we will concern ourselves mainly with the footwork aspect of retreat. The main actions are the half step, multiple skip, spin off and jump spin with the directions being straight, sideways and 45 degree angle.

a) *Half Step:* This is primarily to set your opponent up for a counter. There will be fighters who will aim at you right where you are standing without regard to whether you are going to move or not. This is where the half step comes in. You retreat a half step back or at an angle and your opponent's attack will just fall short of its target. Then you counter. The idea here is to take as small a step as possible and still be safe. Make sure that you don't get any momentum going backward; brace your rear leg just as you set down after the half step so that you can push off and spring forward to counter. Get the concept of your step going backward but your intention to hit still going forward and it will come easily. You can also get the feel of it by doing a half step back and then a lunge forward. Whatever gets the idea across is fine.

1

2

3

4

5

Half step-retreat.

A half step can be applied angling forward, like ships passing in the night, or sideways like a matador letting a bull zoom right by. The actual length of the step will be dictated by necessity but if possible, try not to step so far away as to be out of range to counter. When you angle forward, you can hit as you pass or block.

1

1

2

2

3

3

Half step-angle forward.

Half step-sideways.

b) *Multiple Skip:* This is for getting away from your opponent quickly and with the minimum of effort. Move on the balls of your feet with your head not bobbing up at all and, most of all, be light on your feet. Make as little noise as possible when moving. When you make noise, you are hammering the floor with your feet. You want to zip across the floor, not stomp. No Frankenstein steps allowed. You will get caught and "put to the torch." Get the idea of a flat stone skipping across a lake's surface.

Anywhere along in a skip, you can change directions on your opponent or stop and hit him as he comes in. The half step and multiple skip are easiest done in a line fashion, but are also effective done angularly.

c) *Spin Off:* This foot movement is a side step of sorts and an excellent entry into circling or angular steps. Pivot on your lead foot toward your rear and twist your upper body at the same time. Push off your rear foot to give your pivot a quickness that you will need for evasive action. Then, as you pivot on the lead foot, bring your rear foot around behind you to complete the turn and half step back to complete the entire action.

From here you can keep moving or hold your position and hit. This sudden change of direction is excellent for retreat as it will catch your opponent off guard. This is good against a strong forward charger and is an excellent change-of-direction recovery from your attack.

d) *Jump Spin:* Here is another theoretically unrealistic maneuver; however, I include it here because I have not only worked it myself but have had it worked on me. A tip of the hat goes to Rich Mainenti and Fred King for this one.

Pushing off your lead foot, you turn toward your inside and pivot on your rear foot. During the turn, as you face directly opposite your original facing direction, take your (original) lead foot and spring in the air, still turning, and set it down behind you. As it sets down you pivot and set your rear leg behind you in a stance and you end up sitting in your original stance facing your original direction. Go over the example photos as it is hard to describe this maneuver only with words.

This maneuver is good for surprise and distance. You want to get the feeling of jumping over a small log when you do this. A light and springy feeling is what you are after.

It is quite an odd sight to see your opponent spring away from a clash with you in this manner. I have seen more than one person interrupt an attack because they are shocked by this unorthodox retreat, a good reason to add it to your collection. With the distance covered by this maneuver, you can momentarily create enough space between you and your opponent to reorient yourself or seize the initiative.

All that remains to be said is that your retreat must be speedy, regardless of whether your intention is to set your opponent up, give yourself room to think or just plain run. Scoot, and be quick about it!

1

2

Multiple skip-retreat

3

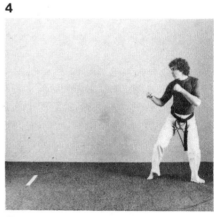

4

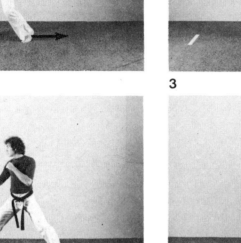

5

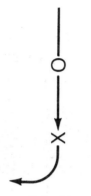

Spin off.

3

1

4

2

5

Spin off-straight punch counter.

40

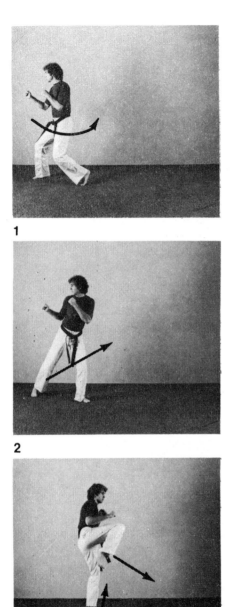

1

2

3

4

5

6

Jump spin.

BODY MOVEMENT WITHOUT FOOTWORK

Body movement without footwork includes a) Rotation and b) Inclination (turning and bending). These body movements are integrated into everything that you do in karate.

Rotation

This is the twisting of the hips and torso. You can either rotate toward your inside or your rear side. Rotations can be used for adding power to your hitting and blocking, positioning your body to shield against a blow, or repositioning a target away from your opponent's attack. Your rotation for a hitting action should be quick and sharp, while a defensive rotation should be quick and relaxed, an easy flowing motion.

The following are examples of offensive rotations. For lead hand attacks you will rotate to your inside, and for rear hand attacks you will rotate to your rear side.

a) *Rotation and Rear Hand Punch:* There are three separate but interlocking actions to this movement:

1) *Rear Leg Push:* The hip twist begins with the straightening of the rear leg. Get the feel of a track sprint runner going out of the starting block. The leg pushes the body forward, not upward, so remember to direct the tension of the rear leg down and back at an angle, not just straight down.

2) *Twisting the Hips:* The most common action of the rear leg pushing off is for the body to lurch forward as in walking, running, etc. Keep the position of the upper body the same as if somebody had his hand on your chest preventing you from going forward an inch. Then as you push off with the rear leg, this will allow you to twist your hips with maximum aid from the leg. As you do this, bend the lead knee slightly and rotate the rear heel outward so that it is aligned with the leg.

3) *Shoulder Rotation and Punch:* During the hip pivot, just as your hips almost square up your opponent (or the direction you are punching), begin the punch and rotate the shoulders so that you end up at an angle to your opponent.

This is in direct opposition to classical karate form. Classical karate form dictates that your shoulders and hips never go beyond being straight on or squared with your opponent. There are several things wrong with this theory: 1) you lose a few inches of reach when you punch and 2) boxers have been doing this method of overturning their shoulders for years with excellent results.

To keep from losing power or balance in this method of twisting, your body must not lean forward or backward or sideways at all. Picture your upper body encased in a greased pipe that is anchored to the wall so that you can do nothing but spin on an axis. Any leaning to the front or side and your balance is going to go so fast you won't have time to recover against your opponent. The whole body and arm recovers back to the fighting position as speedily as possible. The snap back of the arm will naturally be quicker than the body twist.

Practice the hip twist and punch so each move is separate from the rest but in order. When you get the feel of what each part is supposed to do, then interweave the beginning and ending of each separate part so that right before the end of the first move the second move begins, and so on so that it ends up as one flowing motion.

This is the basic idea for every rear hand blow, be it straight punch, round punch, angle hammer or whatever.

The rotation for the lead hand punch will vary for the type of punch you throw. The lead straight punch will require less rotation than the lead round punch.

b) *Lead Straight Punch:* Rotate your shoulders toward your inside and punch with the lead hand and basically you have it. Since the lead fist is tucked in close to the body (one fist width from touching), you need not draw the hand back or twist the hip backward before firing the punch. Keep the elbow under the fist so that it does not flip out sideways and weaken the punch. Roll the shoulders slightly as you punch,

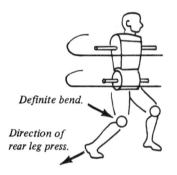

Definite bend.

Direction of rear leg press.

Horizontal body rotation.

1

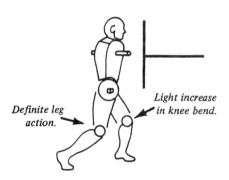

Definite leg action.

Light increase in knee bend.

Maintenance of vertical body position.

2

3

6

4

7

5

8

Rotation-rear hand punch.

1   **2**

Slight rotation-lead straight punch.

but don't end up facing completely sideways as the punch reaches full extension; keep some shoulder angle there.

The lead punch is not a killer blow but, like a boxer's jab, it is a stinger and upsetter. A series of lead jabs thrown in a row tend to confuse the opponent and are good for setting up follow-up attacks.

c) *Lead Round Punch:* The rotation for this punch is fuller than the minimal shoulder roll for the lead straight punch. Rotate by pivoting hips and torso, moving off the balls of the feet. The legs should twist the hips and body around in a sharp motion away from facing your opponent straight on (or slightly angled) to facing your opponent sideways.

Using rotation with an attack after you block is an excellent way to generate a powerful single blow. There was a boxer in the championship days of Jack Johnson that Johnson himself refused to fight, Sam Langford. Sam Langford was a black middleweight who was known for incredibly powerful punching and was avoided by a lot of the top white heavyweight contenders at the time. When asked how he was able to hit so hard, he replied, "I've told you all before. It ain't no secret. It's all in the hips." Classical karate players, boxers, and kick boxers will all tell you the same thing, from hooks to straight shots, it is all in the hips.

Inclination

Inclination is merely bending, forward, sideways, backward or at an angle. This all comes from the waist. You can do this offensively and defensively. It mainly comes into American Karate through the influence of fencing, boxing and some methods of gung fu. Most classically oriented karate methods emphasize a straight up and down posture concerning the upper body.

a) *Offensive Inclination:* Back in 1973–1974, there was a classmate of mine who, rather than use rotation to power his punches, snapped his upper body forward as

1

3

Rotation-lead extended hook (ridge hand).

2

he punched. He was powerfully built so I thought that he could get away without using rotation and still hit hard. Since I was used to rotation-based power it did strike me as odd that he could get as much zing out of his punches as he did. Recently (February 1980) I was listening to another martial artist who was telling me about the four principle revisions Bruce Lee made in the Wing Chun style of gung fu, one of them being shifting from a leg pivot/shoulder rotation method of punching to a snappy, forward body inclination during the punch. Exactly the same thing my classmate was doing unconsciously years before. After testing it out, I found that it was a good deal more powerful than it looked and faster than the rotation method. However, for me, the rotation is more powerful.

The effectiveness of the offensive incline punch lies in its quickness. If you bend and hit, there is no jolt, but if you snap! forward and hit at the same time, you will deliver a shocker. Inclination punching utilizes both momentum and independent unit speed impact for its power.

Use this with a short quick step rather than a long lunge motion. You want to incline not more than 45 degrees and use the body to aid your hitting, not to help you reach your opponent.

46

Inclination (with punch).

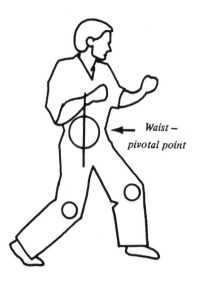

Waist —
pivotal point

Eyes looking up and forward to keep equilibrium.

Waist bend.

Upper body inclination-straight punch.

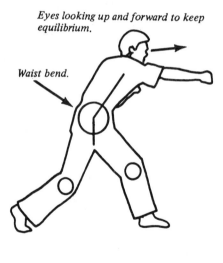

1

2

3

Inclination

b) *Defensive Inclination:* Defensive inclination is merely bending the body in whatever direction so as to avoid an attack. Bending forward you can duck, bob, weave and angle forward or sideways; you can slip or lean and you can lean to the rear. Utilization of these will come later in the book.

DEVELOPING POWER

There are several ways of generating power in your hitting: Rotation/centrifugal force. This is employed in the hip twist method. Momentum. Throwing a body of mass forward so that the weight is added to the muscular power of the hitting unit as in lunge punching. Independent Unit Speed Impact. This is using the maximum speed generated by an independent hitting agent (arm, leg) without using either rotation or momentum. Power Base/Muscular Strength. Anchoring your legs/feet to the floor so that your legs will take up the counter shock resistance of your strike.

Rotation/Centrifugal Force

We went over the mechanics of rotation earlier. Here is the explanation of how it works.

Rotation is the wind up before the punch. Instead of rearing back like a baseball pitcher, the idea here is to fire off a quick twist of the body involving the legs, hips, torso and shoulders at the same instant to generate an explosive take-off for the hitting agent (fist or foot). Almost all karate styles use this type of power development.

Momentum

Momentum is basically throwing your weight around. You throw your weight into your technique to induce follow up, making sure you get there and drive your technique through your opponent.

Independent Unit Speed Impact

This is the raw speed of the technique, how fast it is. It is a well known law of physics that if you double the mass of any given object, you will double its impact, but if you double its velocity (speed) you will quadruple its impact.

This is your basic snapping attack: backfist, round kick, straight punch at times. The Kenpo style here in the United States bases its power on speed impact. Watch a Kenpo player go through a form or partner drill and you will see what I mean. You have to watch out for three points when using a speed impact type of strike:

a) *Snap back* is as important as the snap out. Snap somebody with a towel but don't snap the towel back. It will lose a lot of its zing.

b) *Follow through* about four inches into the target. This is what is different about a powerful speed impact strike and a slapsy smack. You have to follow through. On two separate occasions I have knocked out my opponent with a defensive jumping up lead straight punch. No rotation, no momentum of my own and definitely no power base; just independent unit speed impact and follow through.

c) *Strike at exposed targets.* This type of hit is the one that all of a sudden sets off the tuning fork in your head or sucks the wind right out of you. Sharpness and follow through. Do not punch to the body with a speed impact shot if that shot is going to be muffled by a heavy coat. You do not want to dig with this hit.

Power Base/Muscular Strength

Where momentum can be viewed as the irresistible force, the power base can be looked at as the immovable object. This is where your stance is so solid that when you hit your opponent with a blow, your body position will not give an inch.

Example: If you hit your opponent's body with a punch and he is firmly rooted to the floor and does not move, something will give. If you are up on your toes or have bad balance, your position will give and you will be knocked backward. If your stance is firm, then either your wrist or his body will give.

These are the four basic components of hitting power. Most commonly, three are used together. A stationary rear hand straight punch will use rotation, impact speed and power base; and a lunge rear hand punch will use rotation, momentum and impact speed. Any of the single components can be used together with the exception of momentum and power base. It is rather difficult to plant yourself solidly and move forward at the same time.

TECHNIQUES FOR PUNCHING, KICKING AND BLOCKING

I am only going to give a bare bones description for most of the techniques in this section, outside of blocking, as the actual techniques will not differ much from what is shown in other schools or books. I will point out and explain where there are differences in the way I teach and the accepted norm.

Punching

Usually hand attacks are divided up into two categories: punching (i.e., forefist straight punch) and striking (i.e., backfist strike). To me, any attack with the hand is included under the term punching. It is simpler to categorize that way.

a) *Straight Punch:* On a beginner's first night, I show him the classical method of punching from the hip, centerline punch from the solar plexus and angular straight punch from the shoulder to illustrate the idea of a straight punch. It a) goes straight and b) can be thrown from anywhere. I prefer to use the thumb-up fist position as it is the natural position of the whole arm when hanging. The bones and muscles are aligned naturally and not twisted around. In doing the straight punch, your fist should go straight from the point of origin (hip, shoulder, stance, etc.) to the point of destination (target) with no deviation along its route.

Regardless of origin point, the elbow should be under the fist and not get angled out and away from the body. In fact, the arm should follow the fist. Get the idea of the fist having to travel through a tube or pipe (much like a piston in an engine sliding in a cylinder) and you will get the idea of straightness of the travel route. The punch should pump in and out, fast and straight. I cannot over-emphasize the idea of going straight with your punch. You will lose a lot of power if you door knock, work it off of the elbow. I also emphasize when sparring to punch from the stance; do not cock it back or crank it up before firing. Either have it already in the position you want to punch from or punch from where it already is.

b) *Lunge Punch:* This is the great initial attack and excellent coordination exercise. The trick here is to start the lead foot and the punch at the same time so that you complete the punch and hit your opponent at the fullest rear leg extension in mid-flight. Here is where your momentum is the best.

When doing a single lunge punch, your punching hand will snap back to the basic guard before the whole movement of the lunge has finished. When throwing two punches per lunge, the second punch will land approximately as your lead foot brakes you to a halt. The main thing to remember is to land the initial punch in mid-flight rather than as you brake. You lose all the momentum if you punch late. Also, your hip twist will not be as strong in this but you make up for it with the momentum.

A good exercise for synchronizing the lead foot and punch is to assume the basic fighting stance but put about 75 percent of your weight on the lead foot. Without shifting your weight backward, quickly raise the lead foot, pointing the toes forward, and punch at the same time, but do not push off the rear foot. With all that weight on the lead foot, gravity should pull you forward a bit. Done correctly, you should feel as if a cord has been tied around your wrist and ankle both and jerked forward at the same distance. After you do this enough times to get the feeling of the punching arm and lead leg moving at the same instant, then graduate to the easy step, and then lunge.

c) *Backfist:* As the straight punch is your basic thrusting hand technique, the backfist is your basic snapping technique. You are hitting with the back of the knuckles, snapping the lower arm and using the elbow like a door hinge. The elbow remains stationary as the lower arm fires out and back. This snapping technique relies on speed impact and not driving penetration so it is best to direct it at immediately open targets such as the face, temple, jaw, etc. This shot is to be delivered and returned as fast as possible. To get the feel of the technique, aim your elbow slightly past your target, bringing the fist to your opposite shoulder and then snap it out and back to the same position. When you have the feel for it, shoot it from the basic fighting position or either of the high or low guard positions. You usually use the inclination method of body motion to add power to the strike and can use rotation for a "baseball bat" power shot or for a spin backfist.

d) *Round Punch/Hook:* There are two methods of hook punching; one predominantly uses the arm while the other uses the body to direct the arm.

The extended hook is usually thrown as a ridge hand at arm extension range and the traditional boxers' hook is thrown at close in range, using the body to throw it.

1. *Ridge Hand/Extended Hook:* The ridge hand is thrown by whipping the arm around and hitting with the index knuckle on the inside of the thumb. You have to watch out when throwing this that you do not: a) hit anything solid like the skull, b) keep the thumb tucked far enough under so that you do not injure it, and c) do not drop your hand down and throw it, extend it sideways. The ridge hand attack is good for softer areas such as the throat, temple, and

1

2

3

Straight punch from hip, center and shoulder.

1

2

3

Door knocking.

1

2

3

Lunge punch.

1

2

3

Lunge back fist.

1

3

2

4

Back fist.

1

2

3

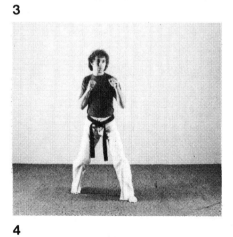

4

5

6

7

Ridge hand.

1

1

2

2

3

3

Hook.

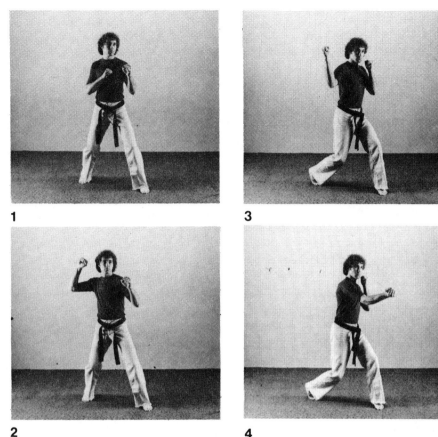

Angle hammer.

jaw. To make it stronger, just ball up your fist and hit with your two front knuckles (this requires a little more bend of the elbow). When you hit with the ridge hand be sure that you keep your elbow at least slightly bent and bounce the hitting agent off the target to get a jolt rather than a dull thud impact.

2. *Boxers' Hook:* This is an excellent close-in punch when done correctly. You want to bring your arm around in a tight bend while rotating in the direction of the punch. The sharper the rotation, the more powerful the punch. Often you drop a slight bit by bending the knees and use an upward push off your legs added to the rotation to increase the power of the hook.

The hook does not necessarily have to come straight across, parallel to the floor. It can come in at all angles, including straight up (upper cut) or straight down (overhand hook). That is one of the things that makes it good for in-fighting.

e) *Angle Hammer:* I include this technique as it is one of the most powerful of the hand techniques. Why it is not more in use in competition is a real mystery to me. You get all of the benefits of rotation based power, the whip of the hook and fairly compact delivery, plus a good amount of power to boot.

From the basic fighting position, let your fist go out from your body while keeping your elbow still close to the ribs. Rotate your body in the direction of your punch and let the fist whip around in a semicircular arc inward. Do this with maximum whip and rotation and hit a bag with it. It is awkward at first but when you coordinate it, you get a tremendous amount of power out of it.

This is a good shot to the side of the head or body and is an excellent substitute for a straight punch if you injure your fist. I used this punch when I broke a bone in the back of my right hand in 1972 and it worked out quite well.

Kicking

Kicking is one of the greatest assets of a karate player. With skill in kicking you can injure an opponent or keep him at a distance. The strength of the legs is a good bit stronger than the arms so the potential power is greater in kicking than punching. Potential is the key word here. Kicking has to be developed to a great degree to be of any use in fighting. Since the arms are far more coordinated than the legs at the beginning stage, you have to give 110 percent of yourself to get anything out of kicking. To become an adequate kicker will take much more training than to be an adequate puncher. Keep that in mind when you feel discouraged with your kicks. They can be great! You just have to keep plugging away.

a) *Front Kick:* This kick is the easiest to learn but one of the hardest to master. Rear Leg: (1) Bring your knee up in front of you, belt high, and foot beside your knee. Your ankle should be bent and toes bent back. (2) Leaving your knee and thigh in that position, use the knee as a door hinge and snap the lower leg out and back to the initial foot-to-knee position. Bend the ankle forward as you snap the foot out so that your leg is basically straight from thigh to the ball of the foot when you strike. Do not lock out the knee joint! Snap the kick back about an inch prior to lock position. Locking the knee joint can damage the joint, so do not lock the kick. The snap back to the knee should be twice as fast as the kick out. (3) Return to the initial stance position.

When snapping the kick back and returning to position, the foot should travel by the knee as it did when kicking out. Do not drop the foot straight to the floor. Keep the standing knee bent and foot flat on the floor. You may pivot the standing foot outward slightly as you begin the kick so that your hips will be aligned as you kick. Do not use your body or arms in a jerking fashion to help the leg up and out. Just pivot and use the leg to kick.

Lead Leg: (1) Lower the heel and rest your weight on your back leg and do steps (1), (2) and (3) of the rear leg kick. Maintain your balance so that you do not fall back to the floor, but rather set the foot down when you want. This is done by placing your hips directly over your supporting foot.

When you kick with the rear leg and set down forward, shift the rear hand forward as you kick, remembering that the lead hand and leg are the same at all times. Make sure that you do not overdo the forward momentum or you will fall forward into the stance.

b) *Angle Kick:* This is a variation of the front kick. It is used to attack at an off angle but not commit you to as big a turn as in the round kick. When you do the kick itself, you do your basic front kick but the lower leg is out away from your support leg about six inches to a foot. This way your kick comes in slightly angled. If you picture your opponent standing totally sideways to you and you want to front kick him in the stomach you will get the basic idea. This is an excellent kick to set up for follow-up punches. It is predominantly a rear leg kick, but is a good lead leg lunge kick to the groin also.

c) *Side Facing Kicks:* There are two methods of side facing kicks that I teach to beginners to get the feel of the kicking actions: the orthodox round kick and the side thrust kick. Later on, when coordination is of a higher order, the Bill Wallace method is introduced. The Wallace method is firing the three basic side facing kicks: round kick, side kick and hook kick, from the same cocking position.

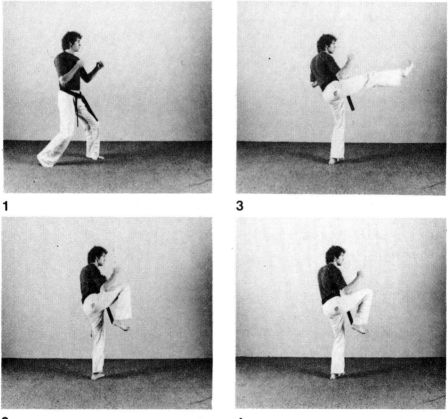

1

2

3

4

Rear leg front kick.

58

1

2

3

4

5

Lead leg front kick.

1

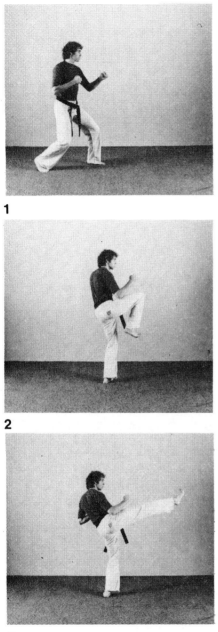

2

3

4

5

Rear leg front kick and set forward.

1

Angle kick.

2

3

The ability to interchange the orthodox and Wallace methods will lead to increased skill in kicking and unpredictability in your own movements.

1. *Orthodox Method*

Round Kick: The round kick is the backfist of kicking. You aim your knee slightly past your target and then hold the knee stationary as your lower leg snaps out and back. Prior to kicking, the foot and knee are the same height, parallel to the floor. It is a front kick that is turned on its side. The striking surface is the instep if you kick to the side of your opponent, and the ball of the foot if you kick to the front. It all depends on the angle of entry. The round kick is a speed impact blow so the snap out and back must be very fast.

Side Thrust Kick: This type of kick is a thrust kick. Basically it is a foot version of the straight punch. Snap kicks work off the knee and are foot versions of the backfist. When doing a thrust kick, keep your attention on the hitting agent, the foot, throughout the kick. Aim it at the target and make sure it travels in a straight line toward its target.

From a side facing position, and with the support leg in full pivot away from the

1

2

3

4

Round kick.

direction of the kick, keep the knee down and begin raising the foot up sideways until it bypasses the knee. When it passes the knee, begin raising the knee and thigh up until it is at least parallel to the floor, with the foot slightly higher. Your foot should be in line with your lead hip and your target, the knee and thigh tucked back toward your upper body. Use the thigh muscles and direct the heel/edge of the foot (blade) straight at your target. Return the kick by pulling back with the knee and thigh.

In the side thrust kick, I cannot over emphasize the importance of using the thigh to propel the kick. It makes the difference between night and day with the kick.

The side thrust kick is a direct power blow. The tendency sometimes is to shove with this kick. Unless you do not wish to hurt your opponent or merely push them away, hit them with a jolt. When hitting the bag with a side thrust kick, make the bag jump, not fly backward. If it flies, you are probably pushing.

Back Kick: The back kick is not a side facing kick, but the mechanics of it and

1

2

3

4

5

6

Side thrust kick.

1

3

2

4

Back kick.

the side thrust kick are almost identical, so I include it right after the side kick explanation.

Look over the same shoulder as the kicking leg. Tuck the foot up close to the back of the thigh, under the butt. As you kick back, incline your body forward, still looking over your shoulder. Direct the heel of your foot straight back, keeping the knee under the foot at all times. At full extension, bring the knee back beside the support leg so the kick from start to finish is done in a pump action.

Watch out for:

1) Hooking the kick. There is a tendency to not work the thigh into this kick and to do most of the kick with the lower leg. This will resemble an upside down front kick.

2) Hitting with the toes/ball of the foot. The striking surface is the heel. The foot can either point down or sideways but hit with the heel.

3) Don't let the knee drift sideways. This will open you for a groin kick. Keep the knee under the foot.

4) Don't pull the kick back with the knee.

2. *Bill Wallace Method - Side Facing Kicks:* Firing different types of kicks from the same position is an innovation by Bill Wallace. Wallace is the most famous kicker in American Karate history. He was rated #1 in point competition and won the Professional Karate Association's middleweight full contact title in 1974. It is ironic that Wallace, whose nickname is "Super Foot," originally came from a karate style that did not kick above the waist.

Prekick Position: The positioning of the body is straight sideways; hipbone, shoulder and lead foot in alignment. Bring the knee and foot up, keeping the foot in line with the butt. The upper body should be protected by the knee and shin and the foot out from the body. The knee, on the side and hook kick, should be quite a bit higher than the foot and both should be as high as possible. On the round kick, the knee and foot should be at the same height. Lean the body back and definitely do not tuck forward toward the kicking leg. Also, turn the ankle in and bend the toes back so that the edge (blade) of the foot is facing your opponent.

From the Cocking Position - Round Kick: Pivot your ankle so that you are circling your foot from a blade facing to instep facing position. Use that circular motion to begin the circling of your lower leg into a parallel position to the floor. From there, snap the kick like a front kick turned on its side, from the knee out and strike with the instep. The kick travels sideways through the air, not at an upward angle.

Straight Side Kick: Extend the foot straight toward your target, using only your leg to do the action. Upon completion, let your leg snap back to the original position. The key points to this kick are:

   a. Keep the knee somewhat stationary. Hinge the lower leg off the knee doing the kick in a snapping motion.
   b. Keep the foot traveling in a straight line toward your opponent. This kick is easy to do like a round kick. The leg snaps out from under the knee, not beside it as in a round kick.
   c. Don't lock out the knee joint.
   d. Don't throw your hips into the kick after starting it.

The reason I call this a side straight kick instead of a side snap kick is that when

1

2

3

4

Wallace method-round kick.

1

3

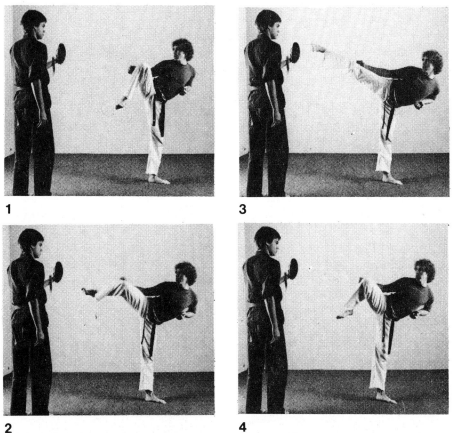

2

4

Wallace method-side kick.

66

1   3

2   4

Wallace method-hook kick.

Pre-kick position for kicks.

1

2

3

4

5

Hook kick.

the leg is in the cocking position, the foot is at about body height and it is easy to shoot straight to the body or slightly upward to the chest. Since I do not fire this type kick to the head and I do not want my students to get into flipping it out without any power, I want them to picture it as a straight kick from the Wallace cocking position, not a flip kick. Wallace made special mention that the side kick in any style is the hardest kick to master. Once you can do this kick skillfully, the others are that much easier to learn.

Hook Kick: Do the straight side kick at an off angle to your opponent. When the leg straightens out, snap the lower leg back like a recoil from a round kick. The thigh moves in the same direction as the heel during the snap back. The idea of a sloppy side kick is what a hook kick turns out to be. You miss your target (side kick wise) and hook back with a bad return (for a side kick) and catch him with your heel.

On All Three Kicks, Keep in Mind:
Raise the knee as high as possible so that you can protect your upper body with your shin.
Keep the foot in a line between you and your target.
Get the idea of raising up and then kicking out. This will keep you from kicking from the floor instead of the cocking position.
Do all of your preliminaries prior to the kick: positioning, pivot, body inclination, etc. Kick with the leg, not with the body.
These are basically snapping kicks, not lock out kicks, so keep them loose and relaxed. Use all of the potential leg action that you can get.
Whatever footwork type you use for entry into the kick, make it a light and quick step. Remember, in both the orthodox and Wallace method kicks, get your preliminaries done before firing the kick to avoid finishing them during the kick. With rear leg kicks, get the idea of turn and kick and basically you will have it. Do your prior positioning and cocking with minimum motion; especially do not use your arms to help throw the kick. You need them for hitting and blocking.

Factors in Skilled Kicking
Here are some factors that may help you with your kicking:

a) *Upper body alignment with kick.* This particular problem is prevalent in side facing kicks. Basically, the body should be in a straight line with the completed extension of the kicking leg. What often happens is that a person when kicking will bend his body forward, bending through the stomach when kicking. This creates an unbalanced situation because you want your upper body to counter balance the weight of the extending leg. Bend your body at the side, not the front, directly away from the kick and proper upper body alignment will occur.

b) *Hip alignment with kick (round kick, side kick, hook kick).* The direction of your kick's force has maximum impact when your body is properly aligned and positioned prior to the kick. A lot of people have trouble on their side facing kicks. One of these problems is the lower body positioning prior to the kick. To remedy this,

1

2

1

3

Round kick.

2

Side kick.

1

2

3

4

Rear leg round kick.

lead with your hip bone as if it were hooked to a line and was being pulled. Aim your hip at your opponent and you will be in good hip alignment.

You can test where your own proper hip alignment with your support foot is by doing a simple test; place your support foot, at first, at a right angle to the direction you are kicking and then raise your leg to rib height. If you feel any kind of sideways pull on your leg, then angle out your support foot away from your opponent until you find the position that will not put any kind of pull on your kicking leg. You will notice that the more your support foot points at your opponent, the more you will have a tendency to bend through the waist and the more awkward the kick will be. Inversely, the more you point your support foot away from your opponent, the more you can put your body behind your kicking leg (bending sideways rather than forward) and the better balance you will have.

c) *Hip alignment with supporting leg.* Make sure you are in a good supporting leg pivot position even with your hip in position; an out of line support foot can blow

1

2

4

5

Rear leg side kick.

3

the kick. The foot can be pointed anywhere from directly opposite the kick to 45 degrees in from that position.

The exact pivot position will be determined by where it is comfortable for you when doing the kick technically exact.

d) *Center of gravity alignment.* The prime reason for poor balance in your kicks is that you are not maintaining a good center of gravity. To do this, merely place your butt over your standing foot and bend the supporting knee a little. That is it. When you fall off balance, it is because your butt is not over your foot and your center of gravity is out of alignment for standing and kicking.

e) *Body bend/stretch imbalance.* If you keep your body too straight up and down when kicking, and you are not very loose, your kicks will remain low. If you bend your upper body too much when kicking, your balance and overall support strength will be weak. What you need to do is to find where your level of stretch and level of upper body inclination meet to produce the strongest possible kick for you. The tighter you are, the more bend you will need. The average is about a 45 degree bend.

Body bend

Hip alignment

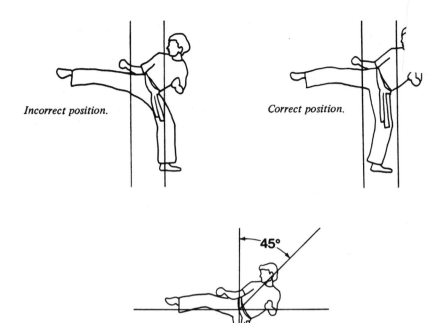

Incorrect position.

Correct position.

45°

Center of gravity alignment

Blocking

Having a water-tight defense is one of my prime considerations in the development of my students. Anybody can walk up and slug someone, but to keep from getting hit is an art in itself. Most modern day karate players concern themselves too much with hitting and not enough with defense work. You can see this at any karate tournament you go to. There are a ton of offensive fighters, but few good counter fighters.

A good defense will even out the balance you need to become a good karate player. In order to have a good defense system, you have to have blocks that actually work and a way of spotting and confronting attacks.

I noticed that when I taught in a karate studio several years back, I taught what was the accepted norm for blocking, forearm blocks, to beginning students. At the same time, when I sparred, I used open hand blocks, much to the dismay of my instructor. It did not make much sense to me to teach one thing and then do what felt natural myself. I have always gone by the premise that if I can do it, anybody can. So, when I started a private class of friends I began to explore, laying out exactly what I did naturally and trying to teach that to my students. I noticed that a lot of my blocking consisted of either guarding my body with my arms or doing what boxers call "picking off blows" with sweeps. Instead of predominantly using my lead arm to block, I was using both arms and I was looking at the actual attack, not at the shoulders or hips. I remembered watching Muhammed Ali many times pick off blows that came at him and his eyes were glued to the actual attacking agents themselves, the hands.

What follows here is what I developed as the defense system I teach now. First the mechanics of blocking and then how to spot and confront the attack itself, which I call monitoring.

The basic idea behind blocking is to either stop or deflect an attack with minimum motion by you. The blocking in American Freestyle Karate consists of motions that are as close to natural reactions as possible. Many karate styles teach forearm blocking but when they spar it quickly turns into a lot of sweeps and guards.

Well, if sweeps and guards come naturally, that is going to be my approach. It is hard enough confronting attacks without adding unwieldy blocking actions to further the mess.

There are primarily three types of actions to blocking: 1) deflection, 2) shielding, and 3) intercepting/stopping.

1. *Deflection:* Sweep, hook (Mantis), downward and backhand blocks. You are knocking an attack off course so that, if completed, it will miss you.
2. *Shielding:* Guards for round kick, hook kick, side kick, hook punch, etc. You place a guard up between your opponent's target and the trajectory of his attack. The guard is as close to the body as is feasible for the attack you are guarding against. Example: your guard for the round kick to the body is closer to you than for a round kick to the head.
3. *Intercepting/Stopping:* Pressing or jamming an opponent's attack just as it comes out of chamber position, before it has power enough to do damage. Pressing back fists or leg jamming side kicks are examples of these. You can also jam a kick by using the lead hand to press your opponent's thigh down as he begins to pick it up for a kick. You will have to move forward in order to do this and use this maneuver against lead leg kicks in order to pull it off safely.

Two prime goals in blocking or defensive manners are minimum of motion and maximum efficiency. Minimum of motion - Do not do anything other than the motion required. Maximum efficiency - Make sure the attack is successfully defended against.

Mechanics of Blocking: The actual number of blocks that I teach are relatively few, again, primarily sweeps and guards.

a) *Deflection Blocks:*
1. Sweep Block: I teach three directions of sweep block: horizontal-straight across, downward angular and straight down.

Horizontal: I just call this a sweep block. You take your open hand, fingers straight up and thumb tucked into the side and move it from one side of your body to the other. Only from one side to the other - any further and you are over-blocking. Once you get to one side and there is no more of you to hit, there is no reason to

Preparatory position for sweeps.

Straight downward sweep.

Upward angle sweep.

Downward angular sweep.

Horizontal sweep.

continue the block. You make contact with the palm, not the palm heel, edge or fingers. It should be a relaxed, easy motion.

You want to watch out for 1) curling the fingers into a grab and 2) keeping the elbow stationary and slapping down; the windshield wiper effect. Your elbow and arm follow the hand and the hand goes straight across. The horizontal sweep is good for zone 1 target defense, head down to just above the solar plexus. I will explain later how I define my target zones.

Downward Angular: I call this an angle sweep. This is done like the straight sweep except it goes downward and slightly away from your body. You go from the same side ribs to the opposite side hip bone. Again, do not block past the body. This is for blocking attacks to the solar plexus to about belt line.

Straight Down: Here you sweep in a straight line to the floor for abdomen and groin attacks. The idea here is to get from point A (hand position) to point B (completed sweep) in as short a route as possible.

Here I am going to break in on the mechanics of blocking to explain my method of targeting. Traditional targeting divides the body into sectional parts: head, body down to waist line, waist line to groin and legs. I section my target zones by your opponent's blocking potential: zone 1, head to above solar plexus; zone 2, solar plexus to waist; zone 3, abdomen to groin; zone 4, legs.

Here is my reasoning. Look at where the elbow bends in conjunction with the torso. It bends close to the solar plexus. Now take the straight sweep block and start doing blocks from the head down. Do a block and move the hand about four inches down and do another, and so on. When you hit the solar plexus level you will find it quite hard to go straight across. From the head down to the solar plexus, the easiest arm motions to do are upward and sideways motions and below that, straight down pushes or extended arm sideways motions. So, when you set up your opponent, you want to set him up within his range of motion. If you want to hit a certain area, know how he can move his arm to defend that area and then work off it. Hence, my "zoning laws."

Back to blocking. . . .

2. Backhand: The backhand block is the mechanical reverse of a sweep block. It is used when a straight punch to the head gets around to the back side of your arm. It is obvious that you cannot duck your hand under your opponent's arm and bring it around to a palm block with any effective speed at all. Also, it is good for a straight downward hammer to the head or collar bone.

3. Rising Block: This block I do not like much, but it has its uses against a back fist to the head if you counter punch at the same time. You bring your lead hand and forearm upward (with the arm bent at an angle - 90 degrees or so) and twist at the last second, hitting with the outer edge of your forearm. For straight punches, this block is risky and a waste of time, but for a backfist or extremely powerful hook, it is effective. Do not leave the arm up after blocking.

4. Hook/Mantis: This is a zone 2 block and is taken from the Praying Mantis gung fu method. You drop your forearm straight down parallel to the floor and when you touch the punching arm, your wrist curls and hooks the arm and you pull sideways.

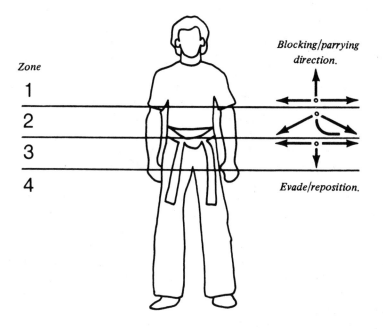

Zone

1

2

3

4

Blocking/parrying direction.

Evade/reposition.

Zoning.

Do not grab with the fingers or continue pushing down after hooking. This is a sideways block, not a straight down or angular one. This is good for straight or uppercut punches to the ribs.

5. Downward Block: This is just a lower version of the hook block for kicks or very low punches. Keep in mind here to connect with the forearm, not the hand. Try to grab a kick over and over with the hand and sooner or later you will jam your fingers so far you will be balling your fist up by your elbow. Again, this is as much of a sideways block as you can manage.

b) *Shielding:* Shielding is placing a guard between your opponent's attack and its intended target. Generally, the closer the guard, the stronger its positioning. This is good for circular attacks and hard to deflect straight ones.

1. High Guard: This is placing your arm up, fist slightly higher than the temple with the elbow foreward and arm straight up and down.

2. Middle Guard: Bend the arm to maximum bend and cover the rib area with it. Rotate your body to position the guard for the attack.

3. Low Guard: Let the upper arm rest alongside the ribs. Bend the elbow and place your fist/wrist beside the groin area. You will have to position it for the trajectory of the kick. Do not just stick it down there and forget about it.

You have to remember that a guard is just that, a guard. It is not a moving deflective action, but a stationary shield. You have to move your body with rotation to move the

Backhand block to the head.

Backhand block to the body.

1

2

→

3

4

Rising block.

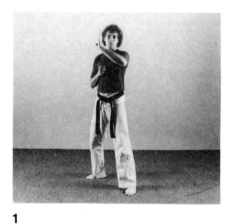

1

3

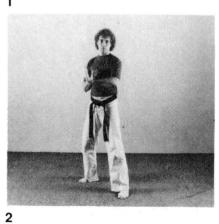

2

4

Hook block.

80

1

1

2

2

3

3

Hook block versus straight punch.

Downward block.

1

High guard.

2

Middle guard.

3

Low guard.

82

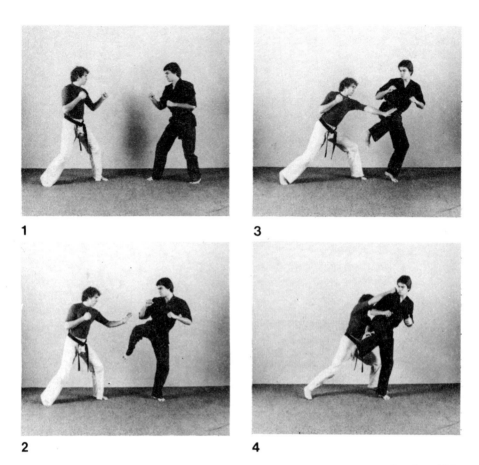

1

2

3

4

Pressing a kick.

guard in the path of the attack. The biggest mistake people make with guards is to stick them up in a position and expect somebody to hit them. Anybody who wants to hit you will find a way past your guard if you just set it there. Rotate for positioning; do not just stick your guard there and forget about it.

    4. Leg Guard: This method of shielding should not be used too many times in succession because of the possibility of your support leg getting swept out from under you. Raise your knee up so that your knee and shin are directly between you and your opponent or in the case of circular kicks, between your opponent's target and the trajectory of your kick. This is also a great place to counter kick from. By no means stand and fight in this position. Use it and be done with it.

    c) *Intercepting/Stopping:* The popular term for interception is "jamming." To jam an attack you have to go forward to meet the attack and stop it before it can generate any power. The two main ways of doing this are pressing and leg checking.

    1. Pressing: Pressing is mainly a stiff arm push to the attacking limb or adjoining section of that limb (shoulder, hip). You can use a press when your opponent ob-

Leg guard.

1

Leg check.

2

Hip check.

3

Hip check versus a spin kick.

telegraphs his attack. Pressing a backfist is about the best use for this move-
ressing a straight punch or extended hook on your opponent's biceps works
theory, but horrible in practice. I do not recommend it.

cking: A leg check is using your foot to obstruct the path of your opponent's kick. This is not a kick to the leg. You put your foot, midshin or lower portion
out in either a front or side kick position and stop your opponent's leg by attaching
your foot to it. "Sticky feet." A variation of this is when your opponent throws a
spin kick. As he spins, you push his butt with your foot. During a spin, you will see
how easy it is to be pushed over. To sharpen your kicking, go from a leg check to a
kick attack and back to a leg check again.

Another variation of this is a hip check. You place your foot in a side kick position on your opponent's hip bone and giving a slight shove. This is great against
people who love to do nothing but kick; they pick up their leg and you push them
away.

MONITORING

With any system of blocking should come a method of attack recognition, a way to tell
what is coming at you. I have found that most karate methods are fairly sketchy on this
point and after all that is said and done, rely upon the student to develop his own intui-
tion. That, to me, is inadequate. There is a definite methodology for the instruction of
every other phase of karate learning but this one. Now, there is one. Get the concept of
what monitoring is and then apply it to your blocking. You can also apply it to your
offensive actions as well.

Monitoring - General Concept

Webster's New Collegiate Dictionary definition, monitor - verb 3, "to watch, observe
or check especially for a special purpose."

Monitoring your opponent is the ability to consciously watch and spot your opponent's
moves as he begins to do them. Most people block as if they were "barricading the fort."
An attack will travel through the air at them and only when it reaches a certain point will
they even begin to block or respond. This is like letting the Indians climb the fort walls
before any action is taken. This comes from a failure to confront the attack itself as it
registers too late to do anything but a last second reaction. Here is where there are wild,
haphazard responses. In other words, the decision to confront and handle the attack
comes too late.

When you monitor your opponent, you are constantly aware of what he is doing at all
times. You monitor the actual attacking agents (fists, feet). When monitoring the attacking agents, you can spot within the first few inches what direction the attack is going to
take and be able to intercept it in flight. It is like putting out your own radar and firing
your own intercepter missiles.

You want to spot your opponent's movements from their point of origin. Point of origin
is the position from which the attack begins. When spotting from the origin point, you

will be able to see what direction the attack will take long before it reaches you; in short, there will be no surprises.

This requires constantly being awake and aware of your opponent. Most karate people are 70 percent asleep when they spar and at times there is up to a 90–100 percent snooze factor. They do not maintain constant attention and awareness of what their opponent is doing and therefore get caught constantly with the same attack or sucker shots. When you are aware of yourself and your opponent, you do not get suckered. It is as simple as that. Just work on staying awake and you will have it in no time.

Monitoring - Technical Approach

There are specific and general monitoring points, depending on your range and opponent's skill. General monitoring points are the shoulders and hips. Movement in these areas will not tell you specifically what attack is coming, but will act as a signal that something is on the way. You cannot punch without the shoulders moving, nor kick without movement from the hips. Operating either on or outside of your opponent's critical distance line is the most effective range you can use for general monitoring points.

Specific monitoring points are the attacking agents themselves: fists and feet. This is where your concentration has to be really acute. If you mentally cut the body in half and monitor your opponent's hands at a point of origin, you will find that he will either move toward or away from the center line you set up. When you divide his body, do it from whatever position he is facing you in; be it front ways, angular or completely sideways. The straight punch is the exception to this; that will move straight at you from the point of origin. The back fist attack will begin with the fist across the center line and the extended hook (ridge hand) will begin by moving out and away from the center line. The downward strike and angle hammer will move up from the point of origin before going downward, and the uppercut, down before going up.

An attack has three parts: point of origin (the starting point); travel route; and point of destination (where he intends to hit).

You want to intercept the attack during its travel, preferably near the middle or three-quarter flight, but definitely not at the end. In order to do this, you have to (1) monitor the point of origin closely to tell what the attack is and where it's targeted (you should be able to tell within the first five inches of travel), and (2) start your block soon enough.

You want to begin your blocking action as he does his attack. Most people do not start to block until an attack gets so close to them that it is too late. They will sleep through the initial stages of an attack and will not realize that one is coming until it is too late. Proper monitoring and good timing on blocking will cut this down by quite a bit.

Next, to make blocking more simple, do what I call "same siding." You assign your hands to handle the attack on whatever side it comes on. Left hand for left side, right hand for right side. (When I say side, I mean your side. Their right straight punch will come off your left side so left block it.) Here you train yourself to block with either hand. Same siding is my recommended method of blocking, although there will be instances where you will have to cross block. Same siding will take care of the confusion of "which arm shall I block this with?" The exception to this is with the side kick. On a side kick, there is no left or right side, just front and rear. In the round and hook kicks, they will

1

2

3

Monitoring

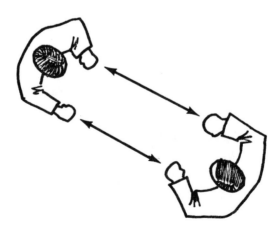

Same siding.

come from the right or left side. With a front kick, it will come from the left or right side of the attacker's body.

The side kick comes straight at you from the center so you can take it with either a lead or rear hand or a guard.

Most people's defenses are less than efficient, at best, because (1) they have been pushed into fast sparring too soon, (2) they have been taught robot-like motions for blocking, (3) they have not been taught how to spot an attack, and (4) they fail to confront the attack itself.

Now we have a method of spotting the attack, monitoring, and easy blocking movements that are more natural motions. All it will take is the proper head work and physical work and the rest will follow.

In order to block with 100 percent effectiveness, you have to do it in this order:

a) Monitor the attacking agents, reach forward and focus. Mentally you go forward to meet the attack, you focus and recognize as he moves. With his being out of range, that is at least a reach of 2½ to 3 feet. The idea of reaching is to actually go out and meet the attack. On the sweeps you go slightly forward with your hand as well as sideways angularly or down. Do not over reach, just reach and intercept.

b) Spot the attack and travel route within the first five inches.

c) Intercept the attack in its travel route, between its point of origin and point of destination.

Focus intently on the hands of your opponent and know at all times where your hands are.

I came across a problem I was having during my own sparring; actually two problems. One, I was getting sucker shots by my own students and was inefficiently covering while attacking. I was getting hit as I moved or was blocked and countered. I came up with an idea. Most of the time while attacking, I focused on my target area, diverting attention from my opponent's attacking agents. I decided to monitor the attacking agents 100

1

2

Either hand blocking a side kick.

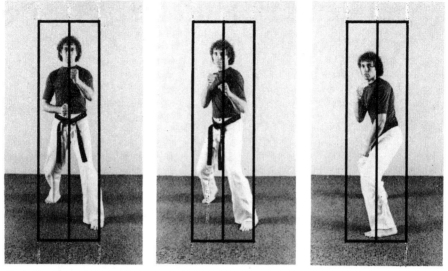

Centerline for various positions.

percent and develop a feel for my target areas, seeing them in the periphery of my vision but definitely not focusing my attention on them. The idea actually is seeing without looking.

Initially, this is a strange thing to do, looking only at the hands, but a few interesting phenomena did occur. By watching the hands, most obviously, you are focusing on your opponent better and are better prepared for his attacks, but more interestingly, you are much better prepared for his counter attacks. I found that after a while, just by a tight monitor on his hands, I could gauge the range of his kicking by the length of his arm range. While watching the hands I could still spot telltale thigh movement prior to my opponent kicking. I could easily tell if a kick or punch was coming and it was easier to see the fake and real attacks. Adjustments in my range were easier to make, especially when I was moving. The most interesting phenomenon was that of reaching over the guard. I had been having trouble hitting anybody with a back fist for a long time, but in a flash the idea of reaching out over the guard came to me. I scored about ten out of twelve back fists, with both hands. This can extend to reaching through the guard, under the guard, maybe around the guard and possibly lifting the guard.

All in all, it has so far proven effective. Use it in conjunction with footwork and work it in both offense and defense.

PRIMARY AND SECONDARY BLOCKS FOR TECHNIQUES

In conjunction with monitoring, these are the recommended set of defensive actions for various techniques. The primary blocks are the ones I find most useful for defense and the secondary blocks are just in case actions. Blocking actions for techniques should by no means be rigidly set. *The situation always dictates the response.* Here is a list of the various defensive actions for offensive techniques. I will include notes on certain techniques as you go down the list.

Straight Punch
Head (1) Sweep (2) Backhand, Rising
Chest (1) Sweep (2) Backhand
Lower Body (1) Angle Sweep (2) Hook, Straight Down
Groin (1) Straight Down, Downward Block
(Straight down is a sweep and downward block, and hook.)

Backfist
Head (1) Same Side Press, (2) Lead Guard, Rising Block
Body (1) Guard
Groin (1) Guard, Downward

Extended Hook (Ridge Hand)
Head (1) Guard (2) Rising (same side)
Body (1) Guard
Groin (1) Guard, Downward

Angle Hammer
Head (1) Guard (2) Sweep, Rising
Body (1) Guard
Groin (1) Hook, Downward

Uppercut
Head (1) Sweep
Body (1) Sweep, Hook (2) Angle Sweep
Groin (1) Hook, Downward

Front Kick
Head (1) Sweep
Chest (1) Sweep
Lower Body (1) Downward (2) Angle Sweep
Groin (1) Downward

Angle and Round Kick
Head (1) Guard (2) Sweep, Rising
Body (1) Guard
Groin (1) Guard (2) Downward

The round kick can be jammed by moving in to meet the direction of the kick. Here you stop the kick before it gathers any power. Same for the hook kick and the side kick, jamming it with a guard. You can intercept a lead leg round kick to the head with an opposite side sweep as the objective of the kick is not a drive through power shot, but a speed impact shot. Therefore, its follow-through should not break through the sweep.

Back Kick

    Head (1) Sweep

    Body (1) Guard, Sweep (2) Downward, Hook

    Groin (1) Straight Down, Downward

The primary actions are done on the same side (except for the body guard) as the back kick has a tendency to angle rather than go straight back.

Side Kick

    Head (1) Sweep

    Body (1) Sweep, Guard (2) Hook

    Groin (1) Straight Down, Downward

The side kick comes straight at you not from a left-right origin point but a forward-back position so with exception of the body guard and hook, the option is yours whether to do a lead or rear hand blocking action. The body guard and hook are done with the lead arm.

Hook Kick

    Head (1) Guard (2) Rising

    Body (1) Guard

    Groin (1) Guard (2) Downward

Axe Kick

    Head, Collar Bone (1) Sweep (2) Back Fist

The axe kick (not demonstrated) is a foot version of the downward hammer fist punch. Go over the list for various techniques and see what feels right for you.

Single Arm Blocking

This is a secondary method of defense. The method of blocking I prefer is a two-armed method; however, most karate players are one-armed bandits when it comes to blocking. Blocking is taught predominantly using the lead arm. Every so often there are certain moves for which the rear arm will be used, but not often. When you use mainly the lead arm for blocking, your opponent's possibilities to set you up for an attack are much greater than if you use two arms.

There are times when you can only block realistically with the lead arm, such as in a side stance. So, I have a way of one-arm blocking for this. This method owes quite a bit to the wing chun gung fu method.

Guard Preparation—Sideways

Your lead elbow is in front of your ribs and your fist is in a line directly between your opponent's and your nose. The fist is about chin high.

Guard Preparation—Frontwards

Your lead elbow is in front of the same side of your ribs and your hand is chin high in a line with your opponent's and your nose.

The idea here is that no matter which way you stand, you have your lead hand and arm in the center of your facing position (center line) and directly pointed at your opponent's face. This puts up an obstruction in the dead center of your body and in order to straight punch you, your opponent has to go over, under or around your arm. If he has to bypass your lead arm, the attack is that much more telegraphed. Monitor him and it is going to be quite easy. For hooks to your inside body and groin you will have to same side guard because the lead arm cannot get into a realistic block or guard position for that attack to those targets.

Your usage of the backhand block, hook block and straight down sweep will come more into play than usual. There is another motion that you can use, "twisting forearm drop." Here, you drop your lead elbow to your body while giving the forearm and upper body a slight twist to your inside. This can be used for a zone 2 straight punch or uppercut.

Doing a one-armed bandit approach will set yourself up to do three types of counter attack possibilities; 1) block with one arm, counter with the other, 2) block and counter with same arm, and 3) simultaneously block and counter. These will all be covered in the defensive approach section of this book.

An added note here: you do not want to block more than three consecutive blocks without either a return attack or totally disengaging from your partner. You can begin to get into a defensive flow that will be hard to pull out of. This holds true for both the two-armed blocking method and the one-armed bandit. Keep it in mind!

MECHANICAL APPROACH— AFTERWORD

This is how I teach and perform the mechanics in my method of American Freestyle Karate. They may or may not differ from how you do them. Try them out; add that which is useful to you and delete that which is not.

OFFENSIVE AND DEFENSIVE APPROACHES

Part one of this book demonstrated the mechanics of offense and defense. Now, part two illustrates how actually to get in there and use them. If your opponent is any good at all, you cannot just walk up and slug him. You will probably get blasted first. This is the reason for different approaches to offense and defense. One of the prime laws of fighting in my method of instruction is:

> The situation dictates the response and/or action taken.

One approach will not work for every kind of fighter. Therefore, you have to tailor your approach to your opponent's weaknesses or habit patterns. True skill is the ability to change and spot change. If you are very good at doing A, B and C and your opponent is a sucker for D but not for A, B or C, what do you do? If you are ready for anything, you will get surprised by nothing and if you can do everything, you will be ready for any situation. Since mechanics from style to style do not vary in great degree, it stands to reason that it is how you get that technique there, the approach, that is important.

Offense: Attack initiated by you either directly or by a setup.

Defense: Working off your opponent's initial actions for your own attack.

I owe a great debt to both Bruce Lee and to Joe Lewis for the categorization of offensive approaches. The offensive approach section is my extrapolation of their categorizations. The categorizations are well set up and cover all entries to offense so I have appropriated them for my use. The defensive section is basically a gradient series of defensive approaches from the most aggressive to least aggressive.

Get a good idea and working knowledge of the offensive and defensive approaches. This quote (one of my favorites, you will see it a few times) from *Omni* magazine, April 1979, truly sums it up. David Levy, International Chess Grand Champion, "The great world chess champion Emmannuel Lasker once said that it is not so much playing the objectively best move that is important as playing the move that is most undesirable for a particular opponent."

RANGE

Your critical distance line (CDL) is established by the extension of your opponent's rear leg toward you in a kick. The point of full extension where he can barely touch you is your CDL *for that opponent*. It is that simple, cut and dried. An easy but bad habit to fall into is going into a "comfort range" with all opponents.

On the average, most of the people you practice with are within a certain height group that varies within five or so inches. It is easy to establish one set range for all. The exceptions to this are, of course, fairly tall or short people.

Falling into a comfort range happens when you turn off your range-monitoring and go on automatic. Then all of a sudden, surprise of surprises, you get nailed by a kick or a punch that you thought was out of range.

Your CDL differs with each opponent. No ifs, ands, or buts!

Stay awake and alert.

The CDL is good for fighting fast opponents, especially if you take a defensive approach. There is a certain range of distance they have to cross prior to being close enough to hit you. If you are awake, you will monitor and be able to spot his telegraph(s) and respond with any number of actions. Offensively, it will give you time to monitor his reactions to your attack.

EFFECTIVE MONITORING RANGE

EMR is also varied by the opponent you face. This is a range inside your CDL but still having a fair amount of safety. Your monitoring has to be very sharp since your opponent has even less range to cross to hit you. This is a good offensive range, conducive to quick, bursting attacks. This range is most effective in a criss-cross position with your opponent (your left foot forward to his right foot forward or reverse). You want to set yourself so that you cut a certain number of his attack possibilities by your position alone and then guarding for the rest. Short people, combining a mobile base with broken rhythm and fully committed entry, can use the EMR to their best attack advantage.

OFFENSIVE APPROACHES

DIRECT ATTACK

Direct attack is your basic singular attack, picking out a target and going for it.

There are several ways you can approach it according to the defensive response of your opponent. For someone who responds to the attack, you can step on his toes, getting extremely close before attacking. For someone who responds to your body movement/ commitment, you need to develop your initial move with or without broken rhythm. For somebody who keeps a good range or constantly moves, either make a great initial move or shift to a different approach.

The best bet for a direct attack is when you can be slightly inside of your opponent's range, as close as possible, so that you do not have much distance to cover to hit him. This is what I call stepping on his toes. Either your opponent does not have a good idea of range or he is going to respond to your technique.

The idea here is that a small action is going to take less time than a large action. Look

1

1

2

Gauging the critical distance line.

2

Example of lunge backfist from the effective monitoring line (EMR).

95

1

2

Example of direct attack-lunge punch from EMR .

1

2

3

Lunge round kick.

at the mechanics involved. Attacker: Decision, gap cross, hit. Defender: Notices attacker's action, action registers, decision, counter action.

How many times have you had this happen? "I knew what the attack was but there was nothing I could do about it." That is because it registered too late for a decision of what to do and implementing the decision. This hinges on the speed of the gap bridge. The faster you cross the gap, the shorter time they have to notice and register the action.

The small action comes in by doing whatever preliminaries prior to the actual attack motion itself so that just before you move, you are in the optimum position. Do your preliminary positioning as part of your mobility so that it is not obvious. If you are going to do a front kick, do not shift from a side to front position one second before you kick. You might as well telephone them and tell them a front kick is coming. Work back and forth from side to angle to front, etc., so that when it fires, it is part of the movement. This way it is a small action. It takes less time to do because in carrying it out it has less step by step parts. Decision - gap cross - hit/kick.

You will get people who will let you slide up or skip extremely close to them without a counter attack because they are waiting for a technique to cue in on. These people are fun to direct attack because they let you step on their toes. This will also work on an opponent who responds by retreating to your commitment. He tries to maintain the same range distance as when you started your commitment so that he can get you to overextend your attack so that he can counter. When you step on his toes, there is no long range, large commitment to counter so you can actually bridge the gap and get close enough to him because he is in a habit of responding to a long range committed action, not a series of small actions (short steps to get close to him). He will move away somewhat uncertain instead of preparing for a counter. (This creeping in on the opponent who responds to a committment will work if your opponent is snoozing and not keeping an alert eye on your movements. It will usually take a large committment to wake him up, an attack alarm clock of sorts.)

A slide up, skip or run step to get in range and then a lunge once in range is probably the quickest way to attack this type of person. Broken rhythm footwork is useful but not as important here as other places because the opponent is responding, remember, to the technique.

You have to take a slightly different approach with an opponent who responds on body movement across the critical distance line. You have to depend on your initial move. You can develop your initial move two ways: synchronize your footwork (lunge in most cases) and your attack to begin at the same time or start the attack slightly before your footwork. In no case should you ever start your footwork first and then attack. The main idea here is to get the attack across the range before your opponent can effectively respond to your body motion. Here it is especially effective to precede your actual attack with false leads, broken rhythm. The idea is to get him confused so that he doesn't know which is the real committed action, and you can time your real attack when he is still recovering from your false lead.

Often your opponent will retreat slightly when you use a standard lunge or slide up entry into a kicking attack so as to overextend you. A good way to foil this and to make up the extra distance is to do a slide up kick action. But prior to the kick itself, add a

1

2

3

4

5

6

Slide up-lunge side kick from the critical distance line (CDL).

lunge off the tail end of the slide up and then kick. You will easily cover the half step your opponent took.

Besides linear entry, you can also put an angle step to good use, especially if you false lead with line steps.

If an opponent keeps his range on you or has a tendency to back off as you try to work your way in, watch out. You are probably up against someone who is familiar with dealing with direct attacks. (This is different from the opponent responding by retreating from a committment. Here you may not be committing yourself to a long range entry across the CDL, and your opponent is responding to the range cross itself, regardless of speed of entry.) A good counter fighter will try to draw his opponent into overreaching his extension so that instead of doing an abrupt, quick action you are suckered into a long commitment and are somewhat off balance. If he keeps his range, *abandon* direct attack and try a different approach.

Final Notes: A direct attack needs full commitment: An explosive take-off, a follow through attack and good timing. It all has to be there without any reservation. If it is not all there, chances are it will not go.

Recommended footwork for punching is the lunge, for kicking, either lunge or skip and for angle kicking, either the lunge or slide up.

The overall options in direct attack are more limited because of the necessity for a small action.

ATTACK BY COMBINATION

"ABC" is merely compounding the direct attack. Here, the initial move is not quite as important, but if you develop it well, your ABC is going to be that much more effective. In ABC, special care should be taken regarding balance so that you can follow up immediately. You have to develop coordination combining forward footwork and good, solid attacks.

When instructing my students up the levels, I divide ABC into three parts: two-blow sparring; follow-ups; and continued fighting in range.

a. *Two-Blow Sparring:* Two-blow sparring is used to bridge the gap between one-blow sparring (white belt stage) and multiple blow sparring (colored belt stage). I do this because I feel that too many white belts are thrown to the lions too soon. They get tossed into multiple blow fast sparring before they are ready. Several months of medium speed two-blow sparring will ease them into being ready for regular sparring. "All in its own good time" is the appropriate cliché for this.

There are four basic mechanical approaches to two-blow sparring: punch-punch, punch-kick, kick-punch, and kick-kick. They can come on your initial attack, after blocking or with a block in between the two attacks. They can be done with the same attacking agent or alternating agents. Also, you can use the same technique or vary the techniques. Here you can already see that within the apparently limited framework there is actually quite a bit to keep a white belt busy for a while.

One of the basic things to watch for in two-blow sparring that applies in almost every approach is the "time lag." A time lag is the amount of time in between one action and the next. The more time there is in between, the greater the time lag. Basically, you want

to avoid having the slightest time lag while keeping the two actions separate.
to do this is when one action is beginning to end, begin the next. This results i
action with two interlocking parts. If you were doing practice in a mirror, you
to end the entire action as you set in your final stance or at full recovery b
original position.

Here are some examples of the possibilities involved with the two-blow format. (Use varying methods of entry, line and angle. These are examples.)

Punch-Punch   **Footwork (Example)**
1. Jab/Back Fist - Reverse Punch   Slide Up
2. Reverse Punch Low - Jab High   Lunge
3. Back Fist Head - Angle Hammer Body   Lunge
4. Ridge Hand Head - Straight Punch Body   Angle Lunge
5. Lead Punch - Rear Lead Back Fist (same hand)

Punch-punch #1

1

2

3

Punch-punch #2

1

2

3

→

4

Punch-punch #3

3

1

4

2

5

Punch-punch #4

102

3

4

1

2

Punch-punch #5

Punch-Kick

1. Jab - Front Kick	Slide Up
2. Back Fist - Round/Side Kick	Skip
3. Reverse Punch - Round Kick (rear leg)	Short Lead Step
4. Ridge Hand - Spin Back Kick	Short Lead Step

1

4

2

5

Punch-kick #1

3

1

2

3

4

5

Punch-kick #2

1

2

3

4

Punch-kick #3

1

2

3

106

4

5

Punch-kick #4

Kick-Punch

1. Round/Side Kick - Back Fist   Lunge
2. Side Kick - Straight Punch   Lunge
3. Angle Kick - Ridge Hand   Rear Leg Kick
4. Spin Back Kick - Back Fist

1

2   →

3

4

Kick-punch # 1

1

3

2

4

Kick-punch #2

1

3

2

4

5

Kick-punch #3

1

2

3

4

5

6

Kick-punch #4

110

Kick-Kick

1. Front Kick - Round Kick   Rear Leg Kick
2. Double Same Type Kick   Slide Up
3. Round Kick - Side Kick   Lunge
4. Side Kick - Spin Back Kick   Skip
5. Side Kick - Angle Kick   Slide Up

1

3

2

4   ⟶

5

6

Kick-kick #1

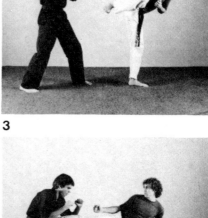

1

3

2

4

Kick-kick #2

112

1

2

3

4

5

6

→

7

Kick-kick #3

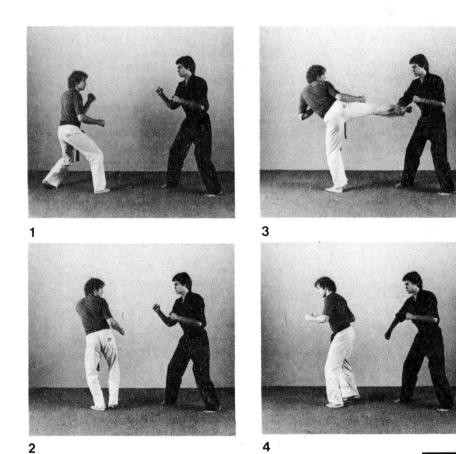

1

2

3

4

114

5

6

Kick-kick #4

1

3

2

4

→

5   6

Both attacks are intended to hit. That is important to remember. The preceding examples can be used for a two-blow entry into Indirect Attack, but more on that later.

Independent Upper Body Action: One point I would like to insert here is the idea of being able to move your upper body regardless of the position of your lower body. In ABC, as well as in indirect attack, there are times when you won't have the time to set the kick (or kick fake) to the floor prior to your follow-up but have to fire the follow-up as soon as possible. Here, your extension has to be without any kind of delay at all. This is what I call "jack knifing," bending the upper body forward sharply so as to be able to reach with your hand attack when your leg is still in the air. You can also use this independent motion idea with blocking a counter attack when a kick is still up. Another method of this same idea is using rotation to pull your body from a side facing kick position to a more front facing position. Rotating into a follow-up punch or block after a round kick or side kick is the easiest for this.

b. *Combinations:* Combination attacks are the logical extensions of two-blow sparring. You enter into a multiple blow combination with a two-blow set-up: hand-hand, hand-foot, foot-hand, foot-foot. Once you are past doing only two-blow sparring, you can divide combinations into two approaches: 1) follow-ups, and 2) continued fighting in range.

Follow-ups are basically chasing an opponent. This is the idea of a "blitz." You take off after an opponent who backs away a lot. Rear leg front kick, straight punch, charging punches and follow-up side kicks are good in this approach. Spin kicks at the end of the follow-up are good also. Basically, you want to chase your opponent with a minimum of twisting and turning; shoot straight forward like an arrow.

One of the classic examples of follow-ups is the "Chuck Norris blitz," which was introduced to me by his student, Bob Barrow. Back in the middle 1960s, Norris became the top tournament competitor by perfecting a series of forward moving combinations. He used an exercise he called "down and back" to perfect his coordination of the attacks and footwork.

"Down and back" merely consists of doing combinations the length of the studio floor,

1

2

3

4

Jack-knifing.

1

2

→

3

4

Independent upper body action rotating from a side position for a punch.

1

3

2

4

Blocking while your kick is still in the air.

with a partner, in a flowing manner with the key being that the footwork never stops. You do not sit dead in a stance; you keep coming on. As your coordination develops in doing this, opportunities will become apparent.

The main reasons behind "blitzing" (rapid charging) an opponent are: 1. closing the gap extremely fast, 2. to physical overwhelm, 3. to surprise, and 4. to gain momentum based power for your attacks.

1. The reason behind this is obvious. The less time spent getting from your out of range position to your opponent, the less time they have to hit you as you come in.
2. You want to hit your opponent with a barrage of shots to different areas of the body so that he cannot possibly block each shot. Also, the feeling of getting struck rapidly and in different areas of the body tends to overwhelm and scatter your opponent (check page on "Randomness").
3. Unexpected, sudden movements cause time lags and hesitancy in your opponent's reaction time and these can be taken advantage of.
4. The more thrust there is in your rear leg in your charge, the more physical mass (momentum) speed you will have; this will replace the loss of power you would have if you were standing in a firmly based stance.

Ninety percent of the success of the blitz depends upon the take-off and thrusting motion of the rear foot. You want to liken the foot work to doing a 100 yard dash in track. You do not pace yourself or build up speed. When the gun goes off, you explode out of the box at a full sprint. Any the less momentum will drastically reduce your chances of scoring.

The main approach for a blitz is a "three-step punch." In the three-step punch blitz, you have to be ready to hit solidly with your second or third punch, depending on how fast your opponent retreats. A rear leg front kick after the punches is a good follow-up.

The main thing you have to watch out for is running into your opponent's counter attack when you chase him down. It is very easy to get caught up into what you are doing and forget that he may stop and hit you.

c. *Continued fighting in range* is where you and your opponent stay inside and "duke it out." Boxing calls this "in-fighting." You continue to attack, block, trip, trap, etc., from a hand range position. Most karate players are used to an extended arm and leg range. So, when someone stays on the inside with them, the first reaction is to defend yourself: "I'm getting hit!" What you want to do is get to a point where you can feel comfortable fighting in range. When you get to that point, you can put the pressure on your opponent and get him on the defensive much easier.

You would be surprised how many karate players downgrade boxers and then absolutely freeze up when backed into a corner. You can only confront that which you are faced with. If you do not get any practice fighting on the inside, you will not be able to deal with it very effectively. If you can keep your opponent at hand or leg range, great! But most street fights take place on the inside, so you have to be ready for this.

With fighting on the inside you need to use knees, elbows, hook and uppercut punches, foot hooks and take downs, clinches, good defensive moving and covering, etc. You can also kick in hand range by doing what I call "tucking kicks." To kick in hand range you have to cock the leg tighter to the body in order to hit with the kick. You must really

1

4

2   *Slide up jab into lead front kick.*

5   *Set down.*

3

6   *Rear angle kick into spin side kick.*

→

7

10

8   *Side spin kick into slide-up side kick.*   **11**

9

12   →

13

16

14   *Set down*

17

15   *Rear hand straight punch into rear leg*
      front kick.

18

Down and back #1

bend the kicking leg to its maximum bend. Front kick, low round kick and side thrust kick are the most easily adaptable to tucking.

When doing combinations you must be able to shift from follow-ups to fighting in range and back, etc. You never know when someone you are chasing down will suddenly plant himself and start to fire back. You do not have that much time to let the realization of what is happening just drift in and settle.

Final Notes: This type of approach is good for street fighting and full contact karate. The idea here is not to get into the "one hit and quit" attitude of point karate. I am not against point karate and, in fact, I really enjoy it, but one must be realistic. Elements of in-fighting such as bobbing and weaving and clinching are techniques that overlap into several approaches (offensive trapping, defensive evasion) and will be covered in their appropriate sections. Be able to execute both single hit and multiple hit sparring as each have their place and can be interchanged on various opponents.

1　　　　　　　　　　*Lunge.*

3

2　　*Low round kick into slide up-side kick.*

4　　　　　　　　　　　　　⟶

123

5

8   *Set down.*

6

9   *Straight punch.*

7

10   *Follow up angle kick into*
                        spinning hook kick.

→

124

11

12

13

14

15   *Follow up with straight punch.*

Down and back #2.

1

2

3

4

5

6

126

7

1

8

2

Three step punch.

3

Tucking front kick.

127

1

1

2

2

3

3

Tucking round kick.

Tucking side kick.

128

1   *Lunge rear straight punch.*

4   *And to the head.*

2   *Double left hook to ribs. . . .*

5

3

6   *Right elbow punch.*

7   *Left tucking front kick.*

10

8

11   *Inside foot hook.*

9

12   *Straight right to the head.*

Continued fighting in range.

INDIRECT ATTACK

Indirect attack consists of using an attention-getter on your opponent. You can either fake an attack, use some sort of distraction or leg sweep. The primary idea is that you are trying to set up an opponent so that he will be in a position where you can hit him or you can work off his natural reaction patterns. When Rocky Graziano was knocked out by Sugar Ray Robinson, his comment to the press was, "I zigged when I shoulda' zagged." This is the idea of what you are doing to your opponent.

Faking

When throwing a fake, you have to establish whether your opponent reacts to a body movement or technique.

Most people do not respond to an independent unit (arm, leg technique) fake, but they do respond to a body fake. This is a generality but is usually the case. You should be able to do both.

Indirect attack is primarily based on faking. A fake is a false lead intended to get your opponent's attention away from your real action. The object of faking is to get the opponent to react *into* the real attack. They will either go for a blocking motion or body motion. You must be able to spot what they do and when.

You want to accomplish two ends when you fake: 1) you must get your opponent going every which way (jumpy) and, 2) you have got to cover distance. When covering distance on a fake, it is the idea of a "half-commitment" which, incidentally, I got from Joe Lewis' articles. Half-committment is merely covering part of the range. Your opponent will never fall for anything that is faked out of range.

There are two basic approaches to faking: faking a technique and faking a body motion. They are often used together.

a. *Technique Faking:* High-Low, Side-Side, Half-Full are the basic approaches to technique faking.

High-Low has to do with up and down faking. You fake high and go low, or fake low and go high. The highs and lows do not necessarily have to be extreme. Example, fake a head punch into a hammer fist to the ribs, etc.

Side-Side is for right-left or left-right movement.

Half-Full is for the same side or broken rhythm techniques, but can be used in conjunction with any of the above.

Any technique fake or set-up can contain any or all of the approaches listed.

The easiest way to learn how to do a fake is to work backward on a technique. Do the full technique, then do it four-fifths, three-fifths, two-fifths and so on until you find the point at which it ceases to look like something to be taken seriously. For that particular opponent, you will have found out how much is needed for them to react. Different opponents will vary in how much of a technique they will react to. A fake should not look like a fake. A fake should look like an attack!

The timing for the follow-up attack on a technique fake is just as his body reacts into the desired position, blam! You fire the real shot. The reason for this is because your opponent has to notice your real attack, it has to register, he has to brake his reaction to your fake and handle the real attack. That is basically driving at 70 m.p.h., hitting the brakes, throwing the car in reverse and peeling out. It is too much in too little time if you

1   *Fake backfist.*

3   *Lunge straight punch, high, low.*

2

4

Technique faking.

1   *Fake body punch.*

2

$\longrightarrow$

3

4 *Lunge backfist, low, high.*

1

3

2 *Fake jab.*

4 *Slide up round kick, side, side.*

1   *Slide up. Fake side kick. . . .*

4

2

5   *Into round kick, low high.*

3

1   *Fake slide up round kick. . . .*

4

2

5

3

6   *Into hook kick combination side, side, low, high.*

135

1

2

3

4

Body faking. Shoulder inclination into round kick.

1

2

3

1

4

2

Fake rotation into back fist.

3

Hip fake-lunge back fist.

1

2

3

4

5

Fake hip rotation into side kick.

138

no time lag in between his reaction and your follow-up. If he goes to a block, do not the block actually touch the fake; that will help it rebound off your arm/leg to block the real attack.

b. *Body Faking:* Here is where you use a sharp motion of the hips or shoulders to appear as if you are attacking. With shoulder fakes, you use inclination and rotation. With hip fakes, you use forward motion or rotation.

The body fake should be the exact action of the attack you are trying to fake. A lot of people will only do a quick lean to fake a backfist while lunging when they throw it for real. Then, they wonder why the person does not fall for the fake. Again, along with the technique fake, work backward to see how much body action is needed to throw off your opponent. Added note: The less motion you need to fake, the more you must put into that motion to approximate a large action. A body action that is four-fifths complete is a larger action than one that is two-fifths complete, so you have to put more energy and zip to make up for the other two-fifths; otherwise it will just look like a small action and not really worth bothering with.

Keep in mind that your opponent has three footwork options to your fakes or attacks: a move forward, hold his position or evade. Use several fakes or safe leads to ascertain just how he reacts so that you make the right move for his reaction. It makes no sense to take a short lead step on somebody who runs or a long lead on someone who moves forward.

Foot Hooks and Sweeps

You can set someone up for an attack by either using "non-technique" distractors or unbalancing actions.

Take-downs and throws are in a different category than foot hooks and sweeps. Take-downs and throws actually get your opponent to the floor while foot hooks and sweeps are unbalancers. A foot hook or sweep is an excellent method of setting up an opponent for a follow-up attack. The prime thing to avoid is putting all your attention on the hook or sweep and forgetting your opponent. This is a great way to get hit as you are coming in. I have worked it quite often and have gotten caught by it also. First, we will go over the mechanics of hooks and sweeps and then into examples.

Look at the direction of pressure in any given stance. Picture a tripod, three legs going down and outward from a central point. The direction of pressure follows the legs out. Look at a stance of a person. People have two legs so balance is a bit more precarious from the start. Now from the central joining point (hips) the legs again go down and outward to the floor. There are two things that keep people from involuntarily sliding to a side split position (not including stretching): 1) the friction from our feet and 2) the combined weight and muscular pressure applied by the legs to make the base more solid.

The outward pressure direction basically follows the thighs and is like two magnets opposing each other.

Now, to unbalance a person, all you need do is to pull his leg in the direction of the outward pressure of his stance. (You would not believe the number of people who bash people in the legs in the name of leg sweeps.)

You want to reduce or completely eliminate the friction of his feet so as to unbalance him. Since it is not feasible to ask him to put powder on the bottoms of his feet, you have

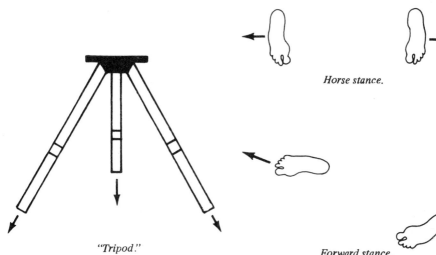

"Tripod."

Horse stance.

Forward stance.

1

3

2

4

Rear leg foot hook, inside.

140

got to hook as close to the foot as possible (ankle) and to jerk as sharply as possible. Curl the foot back toward you so that it resembles a hook.

You also have to have your standing foot no farther away than a shoulder width from his lead foot so you do not lose leverage by being stretched out.

Foot hooks are used against a solid base and foot sweeps are against a mobile base.

A foot sweep is basically used with a slide up, and mechanically it is a slide up round kick or hook kick to the ankle. It is a short snappy action. You can also use a rear leg sweep, but those leave you open for an immediate counter. The idea here is to either turn him slightly or to redirect attention by the slapping of his leg. The less extraneous the movement in this action the better.

a. *Throw/Take-Down*: Get your opponent from a standing position to a prone one.

b. *Foot Hook*: Unbalance opponent from a solid base or when setting down from a kick.

c. *Foot Sweep*: Displace your opponent's position or redirect your opponent's attention while he is mobile.

3

1

4

2

Rear leg foot hook, outside.

Note: I include the description for throwing so as to explain the difference between them and hooks/sweeps. Throwing will be covered in the section on "Attack by Trapping."

d. *Distractions:* Get your opponent's attention. How? I have seen anything from hooting and hollering to the unveiling of an obscene hand signal hidden in the stance. I even worked getting a guy to turn his head and look behind because I stopped fighting and pointed to the stands—in competition, mind you! See what works for you.

Final Notes: An indirect attack works on the premise that you want to redirect your opponent's attention from point A to point B so that you can hit point A. You can use a combination of fakes and hooks/sweeps prior to the real attack. Nowhere in the book of rules does it say just one set-up per attack. This approach is a good one for your imagination so use it.

1

3

2

4

Lead leg foot hook.

1

2

3

4

5

6

Slide up round kick sweep.

1

2

3

4

5

6

Slide up hook kick sweep.

1

4

2

5

3

6

Slide up lead leg foot hook versus jumping opponent.

1

4

2

5

Slide up hook kick sweep versus jumping opponent.

3

ATTACK BY TRAPPING

I divide attack by trapping into two application types: sparring applications and self-defense applications. This is because there are maneuvers that will specifically apply to karate sparring and there are those that will specifically apply to street fighting. It is best to know which will work where.

Example: I was working out with a friend of mine who was extolling the good points of the Wing Chun gung fu method of trapping hands. I told him I had never had it worked on me in sparring. So we sparred, and every time we got in close I pounded him with hooks, knees in the clinches. Then we played with self-defense situations, grabs, attempted punches, etc. He tied my arms up in so many knots I would have sworn he was a sailor. There are situational approaches that are not interchangeable and there are those that are.

A "trap" consists of a grab, arm pin, joint lock, catching a kick or take-down/throw and any type of mat work.

a. *Sparring Applications of Attack by Trapping:* I divide this section into three options: 1) grabbing/pressing, 2) clinching, and 3) take-downs.

1. *Grabbing/Pressing:* This is usually done during your entry into your opponent's range as clinching generally occurs while you are already in range. When you grab you can pull your opponent toward you (or if fighting a heavier opponent, pull yourself to him), turn him, pull up or down. A press is a pushing of the arm either down, sideways or toward the opponent. The idea is to immobilize that attacking agent. This is especially good when immobilizing your opponent's favorite arm. Watch out for extending your arm too far prior to grabbing or pressing because this opens you up. Use the action in conjunction with other arm motions so it is not blatantly obvious. To do this with the feet you can either leg check, hip check, or step on your opponent's foot.

1

2

→

3

4

Example of grabbing

1

3

2

4

Example of pulling into a sidekick

1

2

3

Example of pressing

2. *Clinching:* There are several ways to tie up your opponent so that he cannot hit you with his arms. This is a good way to work on an opponent with knees, elbows, and close hooks on the inside plus a good set-up for going into a take-down.

    a. Two arms over the arms. Here you are putting both your arms over the tops of his arms and applying pressure forward and slightly down. Your wrist and hand curl over his wrist and you tuck your elbows into your body and close to each other. The forearms exert the pressure and the wrists/hands "stick" to your opponent's wrists. You want to make sure that your elbows are in protecting the ribs and that you are hooking, not grabbing with the fingers.

    b. One arm behind the neck, one over the arm. This is a variation of the first, but you hook his neck and pull downward with one arm. Especially keep the elbow in because of your elevated arm position hooking the neck: you will be open for a rib shot if you do not. When your opponent resists your head pull, let him raise his head up, punch him with your other hand and then pull his head back down. This is an effective cheap shot.

    On both clinches a and b you want to start hitting in some way so that your

149

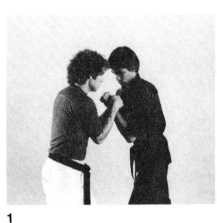

1

Clinch A. Two arms over the arm.

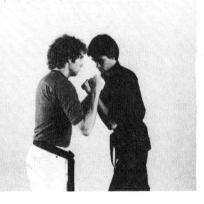

2

3

Sneak punch from a clinch.

150

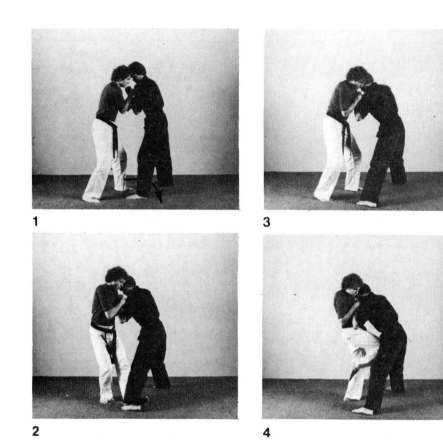

1

2

3

4

Clinch A. Foot hook and knee.

opponent will not disengage and punch you. Knees and low kicks are especially effective for hitting in clinches. You can also disengage yourself and hit coming out of the break.

   c. Both hands behind the neck and pulling down. This was made popular in the second Ali-Frazier boxing match. The first reaction to the head being pulled down is to resist and try to bring yourself upright. Since you can lean your entire weight on his neck, he is expending a lot of wasted energy pulling up. This one is easy to weave out of so you want to counteract that by pumping knees into him or by low kicks. From this clinch you can enter into several chokes or standing immobilizations.

3. *Take-downs:* A take-down is where you end up putting your opponent on the

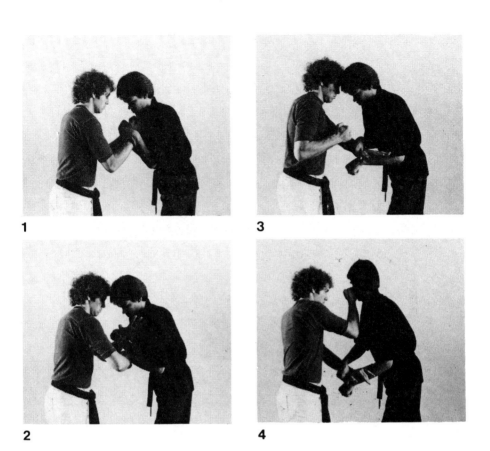

1

2

3

4

Drop your right hand with the downward pressure of your opponent's left. Use your left hand to trap his left and punch over the top.

ground. Judo throws and trips, wrestling take-downs or just picking up somebody and dumping them all come under the concept of take-downs.

Offensively, a take-down should be a follow-up to an attack or fake since it is going to be somewhat risky to try and bridge the gap to do a take-down without getting hit on the way in. Once you are on the inside, you can initiate the take-down action. Defensively, the easiest way to do it is to grab a kick and knock the support leg out from under him. Basically, you want your opponent to over commit himself with a body action so that you can work off it and throw him.

Either way, offensively or defensively, you want to work with their balance rather than attempting to physically up-end them.

Clinch B. One arm behind the neck, one arm over the arm.

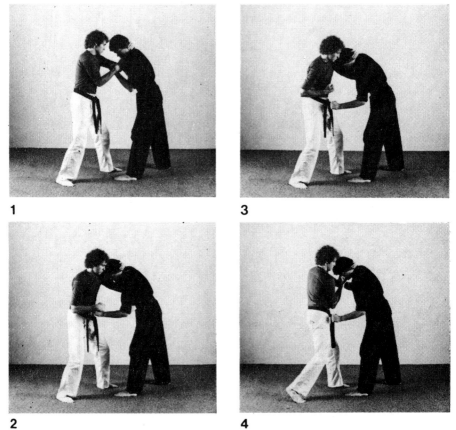

1

3

2

4

Upper cut from Clinch B.

1

4

2

5

Duck your neck under, pull his arm and push up. At the same time, circle your head under and flow up with your knee.

3

Clinch C. Both hands behind the neck and pulling down.

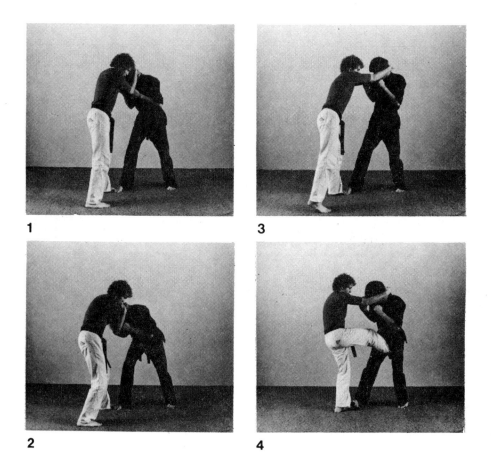

1

2

3

4

Groin kick from Clinch C.

1

2

4

5

3

6

Knee in a takedown from Clinch C.

1

2

3

4

Choke from Clinch C.

Balance In Throwing

I have set up several categories of balance description that I believe are clearer than the usual descriptions. I have especially been dissatisfied with the judo classifications; i.e., hip throws, leg throws, sacrifice throws, etc. Here, I classify throwing/take-downs by method of balance description.

a. *Reposition the mass so that it is out of alignment with the base.* This is exampled best by the basic hip throw, shoulder throw, sommersault throw. Basically the idea here is to get the upper body out of alignment with the stance so that you get an imbalance in the over-all position.

b. *Reposition the mass so that the base no longer provides solid support.* Here what you are doing is repositioning the body weight so that it is mostly supported on one leg. The difference between this and the preceding method is that here your opponent still maintains his balance, albeit on one leg. Then you merely undercut the support leg for the throw. Some opponents will naturally retreat to a one leg position so that you will not have to grapple with them onto one leg.

157

c. *Reposition the base so that it no longer supports the mass.* Here you go directly for the legs without creating any imbalance beforehand. The idea of pulling the rug out from under your opponent is what is employed here. Wrestling's single and double take-downs are examples of this. You have to make sure that you set up your opponent with some kind of distraction so that you do not get hit on the way in.

d. *Getting the body to follow a single extremity.* This is your basic Aikido approach. The main idea is "leading the person around by the nose." A reverse wrist lock and rear choke throw are good examples of these. Any throw involving the head will generally fall under this category.

Natural alignment of body for balance when standing.

Upper body mass out of alignment with base.

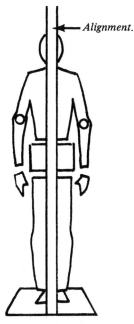

— Alignment.

Base of support (feet)

1

2

3

4

5

Shoulder throw. (Balance in Throwing A.)
Reposition the mass so that it is out of
alignment with the base.

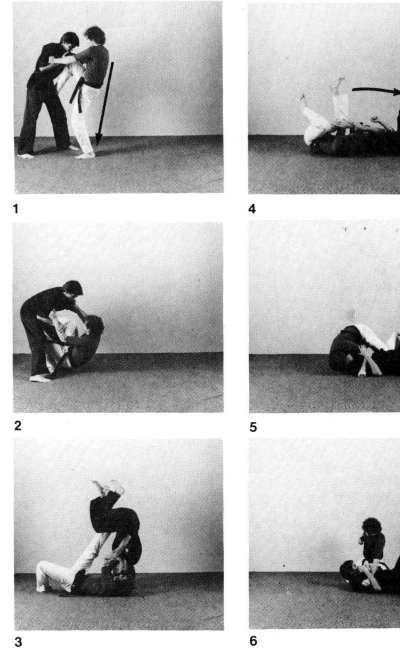

1

2

3

4

5

6

Somersault throw. (Balance in Throwing A.)

1

2

3

4

5

6

Outer reaping throw.(Balance in Throwing B.) Repositioning the mass so that the base no longer provides solid support.

1

2

3

4

5

6

Catching kick and takedown. (Balance in Throwing B.)

1

2

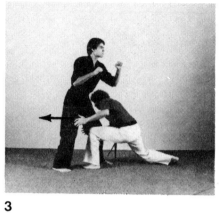

3

4

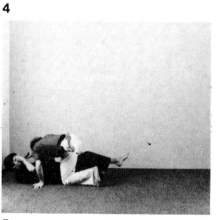

5

Double leg takedown. (Balance in Throwing C.) Repositioning the base so it no longer supports the mass.

1

2

3

4

5

6

Rear leg cut. (Balance in Throwing C.)

1

2

3

4

5

6

Catch kick and twist ankle. (Balance in Throwing D.) Getting the body to follow a single extremity.

1

2

3

4

5

6

Neck twist. (Balance in Throwing D.)

166

Trapping an Overblock

You can set yourself up to do a trap on an opponent who overblocks your attack. When you block, you want to do a blocking action that is just enough for the particular attack. A lot of people overblock, leaving their arm extended, ready to be grabbed, pulled, pressed, etc. Avoid overblocking yourself and capitalize on it when your opponent overblocks.

Basic defensive trapping has to do with either an evade and trap or block and trap approach. Evade and trap tends to be more effective against hand attacks since it is quite difficult to block and trap a punch that is coming at you full speed. If you do block and trap against a punch, it would be more effective to block the punch and go for an immobilization/trap or take-down maneuver involving a different part of the body. It is hard to grab a punch. It is much easier and economical in terms of your energy expenditure to evade the punch and work off the rest of the body. Block and trap is quite effective against single kicks; you just snag them as they touch your blocking arm.

Self-Defense Applications

An explanatory note here. I categorize "self-defense karate" into two sections: 1) fist fighting, and 2) self-defense. Fist fighting is the actual slug out, kicking, punching, clawing, screaming, biting, etc., portion of a fight. Self-defense is against the less aggressive and more annoying type of attack. I feel if you are threatened with bodily harm, then pound the attacker right into the dirt without delay. But there are times when it is not appropriate to pound your opponent, when a simple smack in the face or breakaway will suffice. This is what I term self-defense techniques. There are trapping actions that work better off an arm extension than a punching action. A lot of what I consider self-defense trapping is standard for judo, aikido, jujutsu and some types of gung fu. I will describe examples of the different approach types rather than do an expansive section on the techniques themselves.

a. *Joint Locks:* Arm and wrist. These are your basic immobilization/come alongs that are jujutsu based and adopted by a lot of law enforcement departments in this country. Here you are looking for submission and control, although in extreme cases, they can be used for either dislocating or breaking the joint itself. Judo, jujutsu and aikido books have good examples of joint locks.

b. *Chokes:* Chokes are submission holds designed to render your opponent unconscious. You can approach it two ways: 1) cut off the air supply to the lungs (wind pipe), or 2) cut off blood supply to the brain (carotid artery). Either way is effective although they carry an aspect of danger. When applying a choke you must hit the right spot quickly as your opponent is bound to fight like crazy to get out of it. Any good judo book will have an expansive collection of choke examples.

c. *Grabbing:* This is a lot like the sparring applications, but here you will use a bit more rotation to turn your opponent as you grab him. The reasons for this is that you want to position him for either a shove, take-down or strike of some sort, and since you are defending against (presumably) a non-striking attack, you will have the time to grab *and* rotate rather than on offense when you have to move as fast as possible.

Trapping Hands

This is a method in which you use your opponent's directional arm movement to get him in his own way so as to hinder his own attack possibilities. It generally consists of getting one arm on top of the other and pressing down. Easy as it sounds, it is almost an art in itself and requires a lot of practice. This approach to self-defense is a prominent portion of the Wing Chun gung fu method and its principles have found their way into many other styles. Basically the idea is to tie your opponent up and hit him or immobilize him.

Takedowns

Basically the same ideas apply to self-defense as they do to sparring, but with added emphasis on hitting your opponent before trying to throw him. Unless it is under the optimum balance conditions, do not ever initiate with a take-down without softening up your opponent first. Do not mess around; give the take-down its best chance of working. Soften your opponent up for it first.

ATTACK BY DRAWING

This type of attack approach and the first of the defensive approaches, "Hitting as the Opponent Changes," epitomize the fine art of splitting hairs. Attack by drawing appears defensive and "Hitting as the Opponent Changes" appears offensive. However, if you recheck the definitions for offense and defense I set up in the opening chapter of this section, you will notice that Attack by drawing is an attack after setting up your opponent and "Hitting as the Opponent Changes" is using your opponent's initial action(s) to respond to. 'Tis splitting hairs, I agree, but it works in conjunction with your attitude when fighting, be it offensive or defensive.

There are three approaches to attack by drawing: to draw your opponent by a) "bait," leaving an opening in your guard, b) "push," goad your opponent into attacking prematurely, or c) "pull," pull away out of range and get the opponent to either make up the distance or to chase you.

a. *Bait:* This is fairly simple to do. You merely leave an area open and when your opponent attacks, cover the area or shift its position out of line with the attack. Look for the hole he leaves open as he attacks and go for it. This requires good monitoring and attack recognition to do this well. Note: at times you will have to cover against or actually block his attack as you shoot for the opening.

You can also use stylistic stances and postures to induce someone into attacking. Karate and gung fu have a whole ton of positions that are of minimal use in fighting. Actually, though, any fighting posture you adopt has holes in it and is somewhat of a lure whether you want it to be or not. Accept it and use it to your advantage.

b. *Push:* This requires a bit more trickery. You can goad your opponent with footwork or by pressure. With footwork, you can move in and out of his critical distance line. As you zig-zag his CDL, be ready for him to move on you as you pull out. With pressuring, you can "stutter step" and employ a number of fakes to get the opponent jumpy.

When pressuring your opponent be sure to have noted his favorite attacks and favorite attack positions because when you really get him jumpy, you can expect an attack from him. He will generally fire his attack sooner than he originally wanted, out of nervousness. Monitor him closely. Do not get so caught up with pressuring him that you do not see his attack coming. Get after him, "step on his toes," use broken rhythm, drive him batty, but do not blow it by not monitoring his actions.

c. *Pull:* This is good for driving your opponent somewhat crazy. Basically, you keep stepping out of range or stay totally away from him until his patience breaks and he comes after you full bore. Then you either run or pick him off, depending on what the options are at the time. You can switch back and forth from push to pull to push and really get him going.

Here, make sure that you maintain a water-tight guard, excellent mobility, and a tight monitoring on your opponent to make this work. Your aim is to literally pull him into your attack.

You will notice that you have directional options for drawing your opponent in: moving

1

2

3

4

Jab, trap, and backfist.

forward—push; holding your position—bait; and moving away—pull. Be able to interchange these with the variations in your opponent's approach to best suit your own ends. Also be able to recognize them when they are being pulled on you.

Final Notes: In order to make the offensive (and defensive) approaches work, you have got to give total commitment to them. No half measures will do against anyone who is good at all. When you can do the offensive approaches singularly with some degree of comfort, then compound them. Example #1. Combination attack—Indirect attack. Hit-hit-fake-hit. Example #2. Attack by drawing/Attack by trapping. Bait-block kick-take down-choke.

It is good to have a couple of surprise reserve tactics for when the going gets rough. We all have our favorites; we all should have our backups, too.

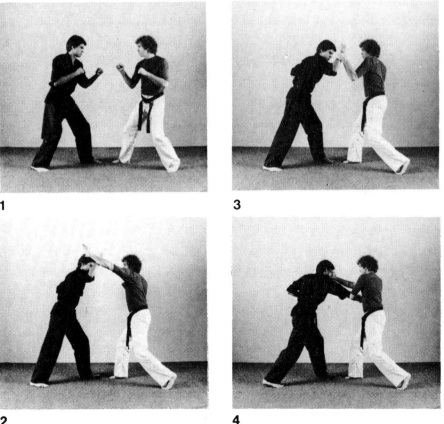

Ridge hand, trap, block, straight punch.

1

2

3

4

5

Duck and double leg takedown.

171

1

2

3

4

5

6

Block, kick and trap (takedown).

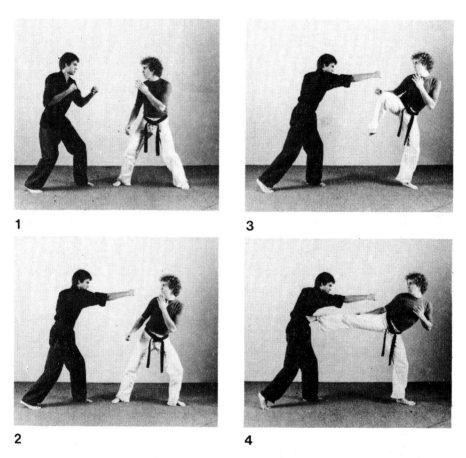

1

2

3

4

Bait your opponent by leaving your head open. Counter with a side kick.

Bait your opponent by leaving your body open. Block the kick and punch.

3

5

4

6

7

Compounding attack approaches, combination attack, indirect attack.

1

4

2

5

Example of compounding attack approaches.
Attack by drawing. Attack by trapping.

3

176

VE APPROACHES

defense is to keep from getting hit. You are responding to your oppo-
mmitment, his taking the initiative, telegraphing or any combination of
he is making the first move and you are working off it. You have three
direction___ _ ons while defending: 1) forward toward your opponent, 2) holding your
position, and 3) away, out of line with your opponent's attack. Different fighters will be
more susceptible to different defensive approaches.

To know all the options you have defensively (as well as offensively) is going to increase
your chances of success against any given opponent. Therefore, get to know these defensive approaches as well as the offensive approaches. You will find they will come in
handy.

Success often hinges on the ability to change. Keep it in mind.

Added Note: Your counter attack type comes under the five offensive approaches.
Most people counter with either a direct attack or combination attack, but you can actually counter with whatever attack approach that is most appropriate.

My #1 rule concerning fighting is: The situation dictates the response!

Nothing *has* to be. There are going to be some responses more optimum than others
but the situation always dictates the response. Often you are not set for the most optimum response, so you have to do what is most appropriate instead. That may be ducking, running, covering or whatever.

Be cautious of using this axiom as an excuse for not being awake and aware of the
opponent and not trying to do your best. It can be the great justifier for chronic mistakes,
bad habits and just plain chickening out. If you are having trouble with an approach,
work with a partner who will give you enough slack so that you can become skilled at it.
Then when the appropriate situation arises, you will be able to handle it.

HIT AS YOUR OPPONENT CHANGES

I put this in the category of defensive approaches because your opponent is moving
first, regardless if he is going to attack or merely moving. Here you want to select a time
to hit your opponent based on his movements. He may be doing footwork or bobbing his
hands or whatever. The main thing is to catch him in mid-move from one point to another. This is good if he is stepping, changing lead legs, dropping an arm, etc. Generally a
direct attack is quite effective in this.

The crucial point is to be ready to attack in a split second without appearing as though
you are ready to pounce. Constantly moving in one place or circling will help disguise
your initial move when you go. Monitor your opponent for lapses, awareness lapses. This
is when to pounce, when he lets his mental guard down. Often it will be when he changes
stances, hand positions, offense to defense, etc. Get in the habit of watching closely and
you will begin to spot the lapses.

HIT AS THE RANGES CROSS

This defensive approach is one of the most effective and somewhat paradoxical of all the defensive approaches. Your opponent is attacking so you go right at him. There is a method to the madness though.

When your opponent attacks, he attacks you in the position you are in at that moment. Assume he has five units of distance to cross before he makes contact; he will time his attack to hit just as he has crossed that fifth unit. When you move forward, you are crossing some of the distance units for him, so now he has only crossed three and is close enough to hit. If you hit as he moves, you will hit him as he is in *mid-move*. Most fighters do not shift mental gears quickly enough to account for the missing distance.

The trick to this is to synchronize your movement forward and attack so that he is moving at the same time. You are timing your attack to land about *in the middle* of the initial distance between you and your opponent. Be sure to cover the target area your

1

2

3

Hit as opponent changes. When the opponent changes hand position by dropping the arm, you punch.

opponent is aiming for or monitor his attacking agent so that you can avoid getting hit by it. Merely hitting him in mid-move is usually enough to upset the power, speed and targeting of his attack, but it is good to be on the safe side by staying alert.

Keep in mind that you are hitting as the *ranges cross,* not as your opponent attacks. If you get this confused with hitting as the opponent attacks, you are opening yourself up for the opponent stepping on your toes and then attacking you from in close. The moment he inches over your critical distance line, go after him. When he attacks he is committing himself, but when he creeps in, he is not. Work off the range, not the commitment.

HOLD YOUR POSITION AND HIT

This is your basic stationary pick-off move. Standing and kicking somebody as they come in is an all-time favorite. So is standing inside of someone's range and counter punching.

The thing you have to keep in mind here is to synchronize your attack with his commitment. You want to catch him coming in. The easiest way to do this is to determine a set distance between you and your opponent and maintain it so that in order for your opponent to hit you, he has to commit himself to a gap-bridging attack action. Then, you hold your ground and hit as he comes in. This illustrates the speed of a smaller action over a larger action.

Example: your opponent lunges in with a backfist. You counter punch. The entire action of your opponent's lunge from out of range and backfist attack involves more body motion than a pivot and counter punch, hence a small action defeating a larger action.

If at all possible, your hold and hit action should be as direct as possible with no preliminary actions other than the counter attack itself. Make sure your preparatory position is such that you can go right from there.

SIMULTANEOUS BLOCK AND HIT

This is where your action requires a block but you want to execute the quickest possible counter, so you hit him at the same time as you block. A person is open every time he throws an attack.

The timing of this is crucial. With monitoring you can spot when your opponent is going to attack. As he attacks, begin your own attack and block (Note: I did not say "block and attack") so that your attack is completed and hits the target just as the block finishes. Shielding an area of your body and hitting at the same time is also part of this concept.

This is used sometimes in competition but is more suited for street fighting. A powerful follow-up is usually used in conjunction with a simultaneous block and hit. Many styles of gung fu emphasize this approach. The key to making this approach work is simplicity. Keep it as easy to work as possible. You can interchange the actual blocking

1

2

3

Five units of distance to cross before making contact.

Hit as the range is crossed. Meet a reverse punch with a jab.

1

2

3

4

5

Hit as the range is crossed. Kick your opponent as he comes in.

181

and hitting agents as the situation demands. This works quite well with both the two-arm and one-arm blocking methods.

A shield and under kick is a guard for a kick and performing a counter kick to the groin underneath. This is great for people who like to kick high a lot. Just bang them low and keep them honest.

BLOCK AND HIT

This is the traditional karate approach to defense and still is a very valid one. It is both quite primitive and sophisticated. The block and hit is strictly a 1-2 move. The tricky

1

2

3

4

Hold and hit with a pick-off side kick.

part of it is in the timing of the counter hit. The counter hit should begin just as the block has knocked the attack off trajectory (sweep, hook, downward block) or stopped the attack (shield and press) so that there is no time lag in between the two movements. The two movements should flow together into one complete movement so that there are no breaks from the start of the block to the return to original position after the attack.

I have found that either holding your position, stepping to an angle or taking a half step back to put your opponent's fully extended technique just inches away from contact to be the preferred footwork for this approach.

EVADE AND HIT/EVADE

Evasion is primarily repositioning the target out of the way of an attack. It can be done with footwork (circling, retreating, jumping, etc). Or it can be done with body movement (ducking, bob and weave, angling, dropping, forward incline and so forth).

Ducking is going under an attack by bending at the waist and the knees. Bobbing is multiple ducking. You duck, begin to rise, change directions and duck again. Weaving is moving side to side in a duck position. To angle forward is to incline forward at an angle to avoid straight shots and get closer to your opponent. A slip is a sideways lean with a slight rotation of the head toward the direction you are leaning. A sideways and backward lean is just leaning away from an attack in those directions.

In evade and hit, the idea is to reposition the body out of the way of an attack but still be in close enough proximity for a counter strike.

Again, you must be monitoring closely so that you can spot the direction of the attack so that you do not dodge only to run right smack into it.

The reason that evade and hit works so nicely is that most fighters do not stay awake and aware of their opponents at all times. They will look at their opponent and their mental camera takes a picture, click, of where you are. It registers, and then they punch at the picture. However, you have moved and by the time this registers, they are committed to the attack and are often tagged on the counter. This is what I mean by inability to shift gears in mid-motion, especially mental gears. You get fixated on your target being in a certain position and you do not change your register of where the target is quickly enough.

Defensive Angling

The primary approach used in defensive angling is to angle past and hit. This can either be done by foot work or by inclination. You want to move yourself, the target area, off the connecting line, but still be in range to return fire. Back in the late 1960s, Joe Lewis introduced the lead angle step forward (inverted body punch counter attack to a kick) in tournament competition. This was the beginning of a whole series of developments on angle stepping. The angle step is great for avoiding head-on collisions with stronger opponents.

Measuring Your Retreat

When you measure your retreat you are using an evasive action to set up your opponent for a counter. Whether you spin off, side step or whatever, you want to keep an eye on your opponent and keep a really good bead on your ranges so that when the moment is right, you are in good position to fire a searing counter.

Lastly, evade. This is one of the best methods of self-defense against an unarmed attacker. It will not do much for building up a tough guy image, but its success rate for pure effectiveness cannot be beaten.

"He who fights and runs away, lives to run another day."

Pogo Possum

1

3

Hold and hit in the effective monitoring range (EMR).

2

1

3

2

4

Simultaneous block and hit.

1

2

Simultaneous block and hit versus the ridge hand.

1 **1**

2 **2**

3 **3**

Simultaneous block and hit versus the back fist.

Simultaneous block and hit versus the round kick.

1

1

2

2

3

3

Simultaneous block and hit versus the angle kick.

Simultaneous block and hit versus the back fist. Here the lead hand is used.

Continuity on a block and hit motion versus a kick.

1

2

3

4

5

Continuity in a block and hit motion versus the back fist.

1

2

4

5

Ducking versus a round kick.

3

1

2

3

4

5

6

7   **8**

Bobbing with a left hook counter.

Final Notes: When taking the counter offensive (counter attacking), remember that this comes in the realm of offensive approaches. Most karate players use a direct attack after a defensive maneuver, but the possibilities are staggering in what you have options for. Example #1. Hit as the ranges cross/attack by trapping. Your opponent throws a backfist attack. As he bridges the gap, you duck and do a double leg take-down. Example #2. Block and hit/indirect attack. Your opponent throws a front kick to your middle. You block and fake a counter backfist to the head. He goes to block the backfist and you side kick under his block.

The possibilities are there. Use your imagination to discover what will fit where. All of these approaches are basic approaches. Do not get so elaborate that your approach has no practical effectiveness, but at the same time, do not get stuck in a rut doing the same thing.

Also, it is a good idea to get into the habit of planning your defense. Set yourself up so that when your opponent attacks, you will be operating through a particular approach mode. You do not want to attempt to specifically second guess what technique he will throw, but just set yourself up so that you will be ready to spot his attack and respond. Check "Orientation Points" for more information. Do this not as the opponent telegraphs or attacks, but in between the exchanges. Then be ready to shift to another approach if the one you choose does not work for the situation. Check pages on "Monitoring" and "Picture Image Recognition" for cross references.

1

2

3

4

5

Weaving under a jab.

1

4

2

5

Angle upper body forward versus a round kick.

3

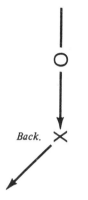

Back.

Forward.

Defensive Angling.

1

2

3

4

Slip left jab with a jab counter.

1

3

2

4

Lead sideways with an angle hammer counter.

1

2

→

196

3

5

4

6

Lean backwards against a kick.

1

2

→

3

4

Upward evasion counter with back fist.

1

3

2

4

Downward evasion with a side drop kick.

1

2

3

4

Upward evasion, jump away side kick.

199

CONCEPTUAL AIDS AND ADDED INFORMATION

This section of the book deals with concepts, ideas and added information. It is said that one picture is worth a thousand words, and in karate instruction, this is true. So here I am going to try to paint some mental pictures to describe some of the ideas following this information. There are many intangibles to sparring, things you cannot use a photograph to illustrate but which are still very important. In fact, to me, these intangibles ("itty bitties" as I call them) are the most important aspects of karate. Small things that make a world of difference; karate is made up of them.

A lot of the following ideas and concepts cover the intangibles.

Much of today's learning leans heavily on the use of pictures and even much of our actual thinking is done in picture form. When someone mentions a warm summer day or a cold glass of water, the imagery comes to mind, not the adjectives, phrases and thousands of words written on the subject, but the imagery based on your own experiences of those things. So now I am going to bring out the mental canvas, brush and oils and paint some intangibles for you. Get the picture?

GRADIENT LEARNING

One of the cornerstones upon which I base my method of instruction is the concept of gradient learning. The basic idea is just to take one step at a time. It is very simple.

Unfortunately, most Americans are of the "gotta do now—gotta have now" frame of mind. In fact, most of today's society is geared toward that concept. The idea is first to build up to a point where you can "do."

Step One

Understanding: learn the technique/approach so that it is understood in your mind. Know what it is you are doing. Have no doubt when you do it and leave no questions unanswered. Anything that is misunderstood in what you learn will sink you quicker than a cement overcoat.

Step Two

Coordination: get the feel of the movement under a non-competitive, no stress atmosphere. Learn how to do the movement right and then do it over and over enough so your body gets the feeling of how it is done correctly. Mirrors and partner practice are great for this. Perform the movement enough so that it becomes an easy, relaxed motion.

Step Three

Placement: start being able to put a technique exactly where you want to. Develop it so that you can place technique with pinpoint accuracy, with maximum muscular control. This way you get out of flinging it to a general area.

Step Four

Coordination in sparring: start to apply the action in a relaxed sparring situation. The main idea here is to not get concerned with scoring. Just do the actions in sparring until they feel comfortable. Get your mind off speed, power, scoring, etc.

From this point, start picking up in speed, power, placement, etc., until you can perform in fast sparring.

*If something is going wrong with any action, you are doing it "out-gradient" to the skill/understanding that you actually possess.

If something is not working, back up, slow down, recheck it step by step. This approach will save you a lot of unnecessary agonized concern. If you are trying to do any action on a higher gradient than you are prepared for, recognize this and back up to a point where you can do it. Then, build from there.

Put the learning of techniques in the same frame of mind as if you were going to learn gymnastics or painting. You are not going on the balance beam until you have your basics, nor are you going to paint anything of worth until you learn the fundamentals of art. It is the same with karate. Do not worry about learning; just take it step by step and it will come.

THE ABILITY TO CONFRONT

"To confront"—verb transitive—Webster's New Collegiate Dictionary 2.a. "to cause to meet: bring face to face."

Psychologically, everything in karate boils right down to the idea of confrontation, to face up to something. Sparring, approaches, technical information, everything.

A person's ability to confront things comes with familiarization and gradient stages of the ability to confront itself.

When you have trouble with any facet of karate, it comes from a failure to confront that particular area. Example: a person is a strong technician and is tough but does not think when sparring. The thing to do is to have them confront thinking during sparring in gradient stages. 1) Plan out each attack and carry out the plan; 2) spot circuits (habit patterns) in your opponent's sparring, etc. Take him through each step until he is up to sparring and thinking.

The ability to confront is such a great part of everything. Anything you can do well is because you can confront it, meet it face to face, nose to nose with a big grin. Karate has always felt easy to me, but acceptance of getting hit in the head has never been easy. My ability to confront things is up on karate and down on getting hit in the head.

Things that you cannot confront easily will have to be worked through, but if you take any one particular thing and work it out in easily handled steps, pretty soon the punch in the head (or whatever) will not seem so awful to you.

This is how I break my students into sparring. Thanks to movies and television, beginners come in with preconceived notions of karate, ranging anywhere from macho brutality to the idea that the studio is a monastic retreat for pacifistic martial monks. But, they have one thing in common: they sit back and tense up when watching somebody else spar. Here it is so close to them, violence, punching faces, kicking groins, struggling. A sparring match can be a fearsome sight to a lot of beginners. So, I start them off easy with a punch, a stance, a kick, a block, until they are comfortable with it. Then slowly, easily in a line drill, they see that attack come at them and block it. Great. That attack was handled. Then after a while, they get into slow and easy, unstructured blocks and attacks with a partner, the same thing that bugged their eyes out in the first place, sparring. The only difference is that through a series of gradient steps, they reached a point where what was once foreign to them was now recognizable and comfortable. That is what the ability to confront is about. Anything you have trouble with, work on in easy steps until it becomes comfortable.

MONITORING

I covered the idea behind monitoring in the blocking section. Here I re-emphasize the importance of it. When you monitor your opponent, you are actually watching him, which means that you are extending your area of concern to include him also.

You have a radius around your body which you are actively monitoring. Have you ever noticed how you do not want someone too close to you when you are talking to them or how you flinch when someone reaches to touch you? They are crossing over this radius, entering your space. Your space has its own dimensions forward, sideways and back. Something foreign can come only so close until it crosses over into being monitored closely.

The idea of monitoring is to expand your space so that it includes your opponent. This way, rather than having an attack cross a certain distance and then be concerned about it, your opponent's very presence in your expanded space merits watching.

Phase two of getting this concept is to accept his presence in your space. Total acceptance is going to calm you down while resistance is going to agitate you. Once you are clam, your overall perception is greater. Do not confuse being calm with becoming lax or lazy. Being calm is merely being devoid of restricting nervous tension. Continue to remain extremely alert to your opponent's actions while not frozen by tension. You will be amazed at what you can see when you have expanded your space to include your opponent and have accepted him into it. Combine this mental feel with the mechanics of monitoring/blocking outlined earlier and you have the entire concept.

CIRCUITS—HABIT PATTERNS

Along with monitoring, spotting circuits is another prime prerequisite to being a skilled fighter. A circuit is an automatic movement, response, etc., that one is not consciously aware of doing or aware of having done. The amount of awareness (or unawareness) varies from technique to technique, and in intensity of unawareness. The term circuit comes from the idea of a computer program. A circuit is programmed and set up to do one function and does not vary from that function. So are habit patterns.

Consider your mind as a computer.

When you first do karate you have to think out each move. You consciously place your feet here, punch there, block this, oops—forgot to counter, etc. You are constantly having to program, feed the computer with what to do now, what to do next and what not to do again. Then as skills progress, there is less conscious effort in the techniques and an easier flow begins to build up. This is a crucial stage and is usually where a circuit begins to form. A technique circuit usually forms following a success or feeling of accomplishment. As you rely on a particular kind of attack or response, there is a tendency to start applying it to most situations, instead of those that are most suited for it.

Let us say a sweep block followed by a straight punch is a technique with which you score often. Each time you score with it, that score is filed and noted on a "score card" in the computer (your mind). The more wins/scores that are associated with that particular technique, the more you use it. The more you use it, the more the particular muscles of the body employed in throwing it get used to it and the more natural it becomes. The more natural it becomes, the more it becomes automatic. When the technique goes on automatic and scores, that is entered on the score card also and that is when you start to get stuck. You have got this computation in the files that says this technique will work on automatic and until that computation is changed, you are stuck in an easily readable circuit.

This also happens when a certain technique feels comfortable and easy to do. People tend to be lazy so that when they respond, the easiest thing to do is what they usually throw. Many techniques have not passed from the difficult stage into the easy stage because of a lack of practicing them. And they are not practiced enough because they are difficult. Hmmmm. . . .

When you are unaware of a technique, block and counter, follow-up, etc., being repetitious (especially being thrown in situations where they do not fit) you are falling into a circuit.

The way to overcome a circuit is to first become consciously aware of the circuit, then be aware of when you fall into it and consciously work to change it. Circuits, at first, generally have to be pointed out by others.

What techniques come easiest to you and what techniques do you use the most? These are prime circuit suspects. Have your classmates and instructor point out whenever you fall into a circuit pattern and when they point one out, work to be aware of it. The hardest circuits to blow are the ones that work the best.

Consider this also. Circuits can be found in all aspects of your sparring. Not only technique circuits, but target circuits (hitting the exact same place on certain techniques), approach circuits, way of thinking circuits, etc. They are all over the place. Watch people and check it out and then check yourself out.

One question often asked is, "Isn't it good to develop some circuits for 'natural reaction'?" In my opinion, no. Circuits are initially set up on the basis of a lazy way to retain an effective move but in that automatic retention, it may pop up at inappropriate times, making it possibly somewhat useless. Do not make excuses for setting up some mental nap time. It's better to be awake and aware.

ATTENTION UNITS—SELF-MONITORING

How is it that so many people get nailed by counter attacks? A simple block and counter seems to be one of the biggies in any type of fighting as far as effectiveness goes. The reason people get tagged with counter attacks is because of stuck attention units.

Assume that you have ten attention units in all. These are actual measurable units that you can place on anything in any amount.

When you throw an attack, your attention is on the attack, usually with the majority of the attention units connected to the attack. That means that you are not necessarily monitoring the opponent with all that much attention. When you miss with the attack, your attention usually follows the attacking agent. How many times have you thrown a rear leg round kick that missed and have spun with it? Following your attack when it misses is a good example of stuck attention units. Your attention is still on the method of hitting even after it missed.

When you go to hit an opponent, do not put all of your attention units on your target. In fact, you should put only as little attention as is needed to find the target and leave the rest free.

This creates the setting for developing a good split focus. You direct your attention at your opponent for good attack possibilities while monitoring him for his counter responses. This is tough to do initially, but an incredible skill by today's standards.

When sparring, besides monitoring your opponent, you have to be able to monitor yourself. How many times have you asked someone, "Wow! That was a good kick! How did you get that in?" And they reply, "I'm not sure." I have had it happen so many times that it is like watching a rerun of an old television show. They do not know how they did what they did. This also applies to why you get hit with the same shot over and over again. If you saw what you did that left you open, you would not do it again. Monitoring yourself is being aware of what you are doing at all times but not necessarily having a rigid control on yourself. Be aware of what you are doing, but do not maintain a tight, rigid control. Rigid control rather than an easy awareness and control is a manifestation of being introverted.

When monitoring yourself, you will be able to tell when mistakes are made and why, how to correct them, etc. All you have to do is watch yourself as well as watch your opponent.

HOW TO THINK WHILE SPARRING

The first thing to do is, again, consider your mind a computer, taking in bits and pieces of data that are fed to it and filed in their appropriate places. What happens to most people is that about 90 percent of what they receive never gets filed and so is lost or gets filed under "miscellaneous garbage."

Now, let's get into appropriate filing rather than losing data.

Monitoring Your Opponent

This is to determine what your opponent is doing so that you can hit him when you want. Most fighters have patterns so glaring that it is almost like being sent a singing telegram. Unfortunately, most fighters are tone deaf. Defensively, what does your opponent do when you fake, attack, do footwork, advance, retreat, jump, stomp, wave your hands, look away, smile, scowl, yell, etc.? Does he retreat, advance, block, hit, cringe, jump, kick, turn, etc.? What does he react with most often? Right hand, left hand, which foot or kick, block and counter, footwork maneuver, etc.?

Most fighters have five or less offensive and defensive patterns that they are comfortable with and use most often.

Do this as an exercise: pick five of your classmates and point out what five reaction patterns they are most comfortable with, in detail to the last degree. What they are doing and how they are doing it. What stance they are in, which side, do they step forward, what hand did they hit with, did they close their eyes? Everything to the smallest detail should be noticed. Position of hands and feet and body, where they can be hit and with what.

You can also do this at tournaments. Style habits are very simple to spot. Look at four or five members of any particular style and see what they respond with to various attacks, etc. They will almost to a 'T' respond the same way.

On offense, how does your opponent attack and from which side? How does he set up for it, what scores for him the most, which hand or foot is it? Does he have any habits prior to throwing it? How close is he, how far?

So you think that this is a lot to remember? Only by looking at these pages and not getting off your butt and actually doing will it be a lot to remember. Once you get into the habit of monitoring your opponent you will find that it will be like taking candy from a baby. It will come that easily. You just have to form the habit of doing it. And then you will be ready for the next part, self-monitoring.

This seems to be the hardest thing for a fighter to do, to look at himself objectively without positive or negative prejudice. Use the criteria set out above and in the following checksheet. Also keep in mind exactly what techniques you get scored on with and all the factors involved. Detached introspection without the usual emotional additives is an excellent guide to mastery of your art.

OBJECTIVE ANALYSIS OF SPARRING

"How to think while sparring" is an excellent lead-in to this.

In my school, we do an exercise in objective analysis of a sparring match. The idea of objective analysis is to view your sparring and your opponent's sparring from a third person detached observer or strategist's point of view. You must give up the subjective viewpoint entirely. Your emotional feelings on a match have nothing to do with the mechanics of it. Your opponent's emotional play within a match can be used against him as part of a strategy.

The first question is "What?" What is going on? Are you winning or losing? What are you doing right and what are you doing wrong with that particular opponent? As your opponents differ in skill, what you are doing right and wrong with each one will differ also. This is also the time to start being meticulous. Almost anyone can spot gross errors; hesitation, being out of range, hitting off target. Start being specific! What is happening with each approach that you try? Are you trying different approaches? What is the pattern of the fight from starting out of range to end of clash?

Once you see what is being done, the next question is "How?" How are you scoring? how is your opponent scoring? How are you keeping from getting hit? How does he set you up when he stands with his left leg forward? Right leg forward? Does he slide up, lunge, fake? How are you hitting him? On what side forward and with what attacking agent and with what attack? Are you blocking, shielding, running, ducking? How is it happening? Are you acting deliberately or instinctively?

Once you know what is happening and how it is being done, the next question is "When?" What is the timing involved? When is the hitting being done? From the beginning of the exchange there are several places where you can hit or get hit: 1) at the beginning. The initial move or defensive move as the opponent moves or as ranges cross; 2) in between your attacks, in the middle of the combination; 3) during a hesitation. Many fighters will score, hesitate in range 1-2-3, then continue. Sometimes the hesitation is not that long, but the hesitation is still there. Sometimes he will quit after he scores and simply meander back out of range; 4) going out of range or defensive footwork.

Find out what general errors you commit, what does everyone hit you with? And then find out specifics. What sucker shots do you get tagged by? What do you tag others with and how do you do it? When you put together the *what, how* and *when* of things you begin to see patterns emerge.

Example: Your opponent scores well on a low groin kick-backfist head combination. *What* is happening? You are both same side forward (left leg to left leg, leading), the opponent throws a groin kick, you respond in a manner to leave open your head and his backfist scores. *How*? In this instance, it is a lead leg lunge round kick. Your lead hand drops to cover a groin shot. Your rear hand does not move or moves insufficiently to cover the head so the backfist scores. *When*? You are both close enough so your opponent can throw the lunge kick with a minimum of telegraphing. As you drop your lead guard to stop the kick, he times the backfist so you cannot raise your guard in time to cover it.

It is that easy. Learn to do it in gradient steps.
1. Watch others spar and apply this method of analysis.
2. Spar slowly and analyze generally.
3. Stop after each exchange and analyze specifically.
4. Do #2 and #3 gradually speeding up.
Do not go past what you can do comfortably.

When people spar they get caught up in the emotional/instinctive part of sparring a good portion of the time. Typical comments: "I guess I was not paying attention . . ." and "I don't remember exactly what happened blow by blow; I was too involved in what was going on."

The great trick to objective analysis in sparring is to be able to analyze while in the heat of the battle. Analyzing before and after sparring is good but definitely lower gradients. What is the reasoning behind objective analysis? To spot circuit patterns and to adjust your approach to work around or off their patterns, the ability to change. One of the greatest abilities of sparring is the ability to change, simply change.

If your opponent does not fight according to your favorite approach, tailor your approach to his greatest number of weaknesses. How, you ask? What, how and when, I answer.

Start actually looking at what you are doing and what your opponent is doing. Get that brain working overtime. When you blindly spar or sleepwalk, the best you can hope for is a good workout and a good time, but you will gain nothing in understanding. Start taxing yourself, start controlling your every move. Do not fight on instinct. That will trip you up at this stage.

Do not do a block, counter, move, kick, etc., unless it is what *you decide* to do. The trick to controlling your opponent is to get him to lose control of what he is doing. Control your own motions and you control the fight.

KNOW WHAT YOU AND YOUR OPPONENT ARE DOING!

"The great world chess champion Emmanuel Lasker once said that it is not so much playing the objectively best move that is important as playing the move that is most undesirable for a particular opponent." David Levy, International Chess Grand Champion, *Omni,* April 1979.

CERTAINTY OF EXPRESSION

I came across this concept when reviewing test results with students of mine. I knew that they had done their homework by talking to them at various times on karate principles and approaches, but when it came time for the test, they were hesitant in expressing, with certainty, their karate knowledge. In application during sparring, the hesitation and uncertainty were there again.

Expression can be either verbal or physical. If a person knows something, he should be able to express it. If you know something, you should be able to do it.

In karate, the degree to which you can describe a particular action, principle or approach is going to parallel your ability to execute it. To describe it to another is a form of certainty of expression. Check it out. The maneuvers you cannot describe are generally the ones you cannot do very well.

The better at verbal expression, the greater the understanding. The greater the understanding, the more skillful the execution. In this type of karate, understanding of what you are doing is of prime importance.

Lack of verbal certainty of expression will manifest itself in uncertain physical expression.

Therefore, number one: do your "knowledge homework." Find out the hows, whys, and whats about every specific technique and approach. Reach a point where you know what you are doing. Number two: work on being able to discuss it with some degree of certainty with your instructor. Most students are hesitant to tell their instructor about a technique, principle, etc., for fear of being incorrect. The reason for becoming educated is so that you will have knowledge and certainty in whatever areas you are being educated in. So learn and feel good about what you have learned. Know it and be certain about it within yourself. When called upon to speak about it, do it with some backing.

TOTAL COMMITMENT

Commitment has to do with attitude. Commitment is the will power behind the action taken to complete any given goal or fulfill a decision made. Partial commitment may succeed in partial completion of a goal; total commitment will succeed at full completion of a goal. It is an attitude. Either you will see a goal through to its completion or you will not. It is that simple.

You can apply this to the mechanics of a sparring match. Why do some attacks score and some do not? Why can some people just walk right up and hit someone?

When you throw a technique or series of techniques, the way you are going to score is by putting as much of yourself into the technique as possible. Techniques or approaches that are hesitant, off target, ill timed, out of range, etc., are basically uncommitted techniques.

To give total commitment to a technique, you have to give it all, body and spirit. Bodywise, you have to deliver it with speed and power, fully cross the range, go for exact targets with razor sharp, precision techniques. Spirit-wise, you have to have full intention, come hell or high water, of completing the desired end result of your action. You develop a tunnel vision of sorts, not allowing even the slightest thing deter you from the approach you make.

When you develop this type of tunnel vision, make sure you do not fall into another type of tunnel vision; one of "nothing exists but the attack." While attacking with total commitment, you still have to monitor your opponent for openings and possible counters.

You have to watch out for falling into two traps, over monitoring and blind commitment. Over monitoring will cause you to put higher consideration on your opponent's attacks than your own. Here is where uncommitted attacks, hesitation, bad timing and placement, etc. occur. You hardly ever hit your opponent because you are too concerned about what he is doing.

Blind commitment is to go in and totally disregard what your opponent is doing. Here is where you get sucker shot and picked off. You are too totally wrapped up in what you yourself are doing to the exclusion of the person you are fighting.

With total commitment, you monitor your opponent so that if he attacks as you come in, you can block or cover while you are still coming in at him.

REACH

Do you ever find yourself out of range in your attacks, especially on a lunge type of footwork? Odds are you are not "reaching." A reach is an extension with the intention of arriving at a predetermined destination. The reason many attacks fall short is because of lack of sufficient reach; the lack of intention to complete the extension. "Well . . . I wanted to hit him . . . I tried . . ." But the commitment was not there.

Let me graphically illustrate reach. I had a student get out of range and do a lunge backfist at my head several times. His fist landed at my head. Then, I took one step back and told him to stand there, just reach out with his hand to my face; not hit, just reach. I took two more steps back and said "Reach! Go ahead if you have to lean on your front foot. Get the feeling of reaching!" Finally, he ended up on one foot, stretching, reaching as far as he could. Then I had him get into range again and this time I said "Backfist at me but this time, reach, with both the backfist and your footwork." He hit me with the forearm and his body ended up right next to mine on the first attempt, without the effort it would have taken before the exercise. Check it out. Reach and it will get there.

AGREEMENT IN SPARRING

Agreement with yourself in sparring is in direct proportion to the amount of confidence you have in your own sparring approaches, techniques, etc. Going out of agreement with yourself and into agreement with your opponent is to place him at a higher level of consideration than yourself. "He can kick better, she is going to beat me, there is no way I can . . ." Most of the time this is what does it. There are times when one is definitely out-classed and overmatched in skill. The thing to do when this happens is to acknowledge it to yourself and not cave in. Keep on sparring with confidence in yourself.

A lot of times what happens is when, let us say, a green belt faces a good black belt, the green belt will cave in and go back to the confidence level he had as a white belt. This is absolutely ridiculous. He is still a green belt. He should act and fight like one and not crumble the first or hundred and first time he is out-classed. You cannot go from point E to point F if you keep falling back to point A all the time. That is the idea of going out of agreement with yourself. In sparring matches, one of the first things you will see is one fighter going into agreement with the other. Often it will switch back and forth many times during a single session.

This has also to do with maintaining a fight plan; the approach you decide on will work on a particular opponent.

Any time you fight another's fight plan, another's principles against your own, you are going way out of agreement with yourself. Can you win by fighting against yourself? Nobody that I know does.

Work out in another school sometime and see if you can fight your fight or if you get sucked into your opponent's. In another school, it is easier to go out of agreement with yourself due to the "mass agreement" of the school. Everybody is performing the same way; i.e., sparring from the same stance, throwing the same techniques, etc.

If you can maintain and make your own approach to fighting work, then you can really fight your fight. And that is what a skilled fighter is all about.

CONTROLLING THE FIGHT (INITIATIVE)

How can you control your opponent? *You cannot!* It is as simple as that! If you can, get him into sitting down on the floor with his back to you so that you can kick him from behind. Or better still, have him hand you a $20.00 bill instead of attacking. If you can do that, you can control your opponent; otherwise you cannot! You can control the tempo and outcome of a match by working around your opponent's patterns and by controlling your own actions and responses to him. This is what I call taking the initiative. Rather than letting happen whatever happens in a non-determinative way, you control what you are going to do.

209

You can take control of a fight by taking the initiative away from the opponent.

This is one of the most talked about ideas in karate with the least workable information distributed. Therefore, everyone talks about it and nobody knows how to do it. Usually, your opponent is trying to control you, trying to get you to react in a method that will allow him to hit you with his favorite shots.

Basically, control of any fight takes place in control of your own responses. You do what you want to do and not what you have to do. If you let your opponent establish the pattern of the fight, against your agreement, then your overall ability to win is impaired.

If your opponent begins to establish the pattern of the fight, the first thing to do is to break contact with him; simply stepping out of range is good enough. Then as you re-establish contact, take the initiative with either unexpected actions or actions contrary to the pattern he set up. Taking the initiative can be anything from a simple stance change to a change in offensive or defensive approach. I have found that using footwork is one of the best ways of taking control of the initiative. If you feel you are getting into a defensive flow, disengage and return.

All you need do is totally control yourself and fight the match the way you want to. Remember that usually every karate player has about five or fewer offensive and defensive patterns and technique approaches that are exclusively used. Discover what they are and act contrary to them.

PICTURE IMAGE RECOGNITION

Picture image recognition is when you recognize an attack or opening in your opponent's guard and give an appropriate response to it. This is what the grand old masters call "oneness." It happens faster than thought process.

When you start out, you use a lot of thought process going through the sparring applications of techniques. You start out slowly enough so that you can think and decide while sparring. As one speeds up, the time used to think and decide becomes shorter and one has to make instant decisions. You will have moments when you "saw" and responded. That is picture image recognition. You saw the opening, hit with the appropriate technique faster than if you had to think about it.

From what I have experienced so far, this happens defensively more often than offensively.

Offensively there is generally the decision to do an action, waiting for an opening or setting up an opening and then implementing the decision (attacking). That does not leave much to spontaneity. Every once in a while, the opening will just suddenly be there and, blam! so will your attack. That is what I am talking about, picture image recognition.

This is just for information. Do not try to work on it. Just recognize and acknowledge it when it happens. Working on ironing out your own circuits and skill at monitoring will enhance your picture image recognition.

If it does not come naturally, it cannot be forced.

If something like this happens but you do not have full awareness of what is happening or what happened, consider it as being a circuit.

With picture image recognition, you will be very aware of what is going on at the time it is happening. This is a truly "natural response."

ORIENTATION POINTS

A lot of indecision and hesitation during sparring comes from a lack of orientation point. For example, have you ever noticed how much simpler everything becomes when you decide to just pick a single approach (i.e., defensive block and hit, offensive direct attack) and follow it in sparring? The more you cut down on your options, the less confusing sparring becomes.

This is because you have chosen to single out a certain approach pattern to "filter" through whatever your opponent does. That becomes your orientation point. A famous karate player, Joe Lewis, calls it "point-of-view."

You can get the idea of this by picturing looking through a red lens at everything. There, the entire color spectrum becomes less diverse because everything is now relating directly through the color red. Everything is red, light red, dark red, etc. Red is your orientation point in regard to color when looking through a red lens. This applies to approaches. You work with one until you feel good at it. Then it is time to add more.

In the beginning, it is good to hold on to orientation points because they give you a point to operate from, a line of reasoning to receive input from. However, as you grow in skill and learning, you have to learn to give up orientation points you feel safe with so you can get good at new ones. There is not a tennis champ right now who is only good on his backhand but poor on his forehand.

Then, once you feel safe with several orientation points, you can work on shifting from one to the next, to the next, etc., until you can change at will.

Most karate people do not progress so that they have several orientation points to choose from. Since all fighters do not fight exactly the same, you cannot work the same approach on every fighter. Adaptability is the key here.

Keep in mind that the only reason that you will cling to a single approach or small number of approaches is to retain a feeling of safety. This viewpoint will only end up with your nose facing into a corner. Become good at an approach, get oriented within that particular framework and then work on another, keeping the one(s) you have in reserve. Pull them out of the closet every once in a while to keep them from getting too much dust on them, but do not get stuck into using only them.

Besides offensive and defensive approaches, you can use this for anything related to sparring, footwork, monitoring, rhythm.

On a stale night, I will go through five or six changes to get into a mode from which I can feel good operating.

Orientation points. The trick is to develop them and then be able to shift when you need to.

One of the best ways to use orientation points is to "plan your defense." Most karate players get nailed by offensive actions rather than by defensive counter actions. This is because when they are squared off with their opponent, they have a tendency to be mentally adrift, or waiting without a plan of action. When all of a sudden an attack comes in, they snap into an automatic response. Usually it is a defensive one, backing up, turning away, freezing up, etc. Every so often it is hitting, but that is not the norm. When you plan your defense, you are orienting your counter action through a specific mode of operations. You are then waiting, monitoring and timing the specifics of how and when to implement the action. Most important, it wakes you up. Since different opponents fight differently, become familiar with different defensive approaches so that you can use the appropriate mode of action for your opponent. Working with orientation points is a primary step to "Operational Modes." Operational modes are made up of a combination of offensive, defensive and rhythmic orientation points to make up one package deal.

OPERATIONAL MODES

Besides monitoring for specific attack and general movement telegraphs, it is good to learn to monitor approach and rhythmic operational modes. Your opponent will orient himself and his attack/defense methods around certain offensive and defensive approaches. The whole package (example: two offensive approaches, one defensive approach, one footwork pattern) is his operational mode. Learning how to recognize this is going to be an asset to you.

For every ploy there is an equally efficient counter ploy. The key here is to be able to recognize what is being used against you and work off that.

Become familiar with the offensive and defensive approaches, so much so that you can spot them immediately. Make a list of the offensive approaches. Which defensive approaches counter each offensive approach in order from maximum efficiency to minimum efficiency? Do the same with offensive approaches against each defensive approach. Then do the same with footwork patterns and rhythm patterns. From there you will find that there is a mode of operation for every opponent you will come up against.

The more familiar you are with approaches, the better you will be able to cope with them. A punch is a punch and a kick is a kick, but they have to get there somehow and that somehow is what you want to be able to spot.

Here again, I go back to using the mind as a computer. You receive data input in the form of recognition of operational modes and you decide on how to handle it on the basis of the information you have stored in your own memory banks, be it from experience or learned data. It is really not so hard to do. You do this kind of thinking when driving, choosing a book, etc. Just get into this frame of thinking and it will come smoothly with time.

RANDOMNESS

Randomness comes from the word random (Webster's New Collegiate Dictionary—random: "without definite aim, direction, rule or method"). It is the application of chaos to an opponent (Webster's New Collegiate Dictionary—chaos: 2.b. "a state of utter confusion").

When you can set a course or method for anything, the less confusing and chaotic that thing becomes. This holds especially true for receiving attacks.

The number of added elements increases the randomness in any given area. Directed randomness acts like an electric current to a circuit. Once the electric current passes the point the circuit can handle, the circuit breaker acts and shuts everything down.

Apply that to your conscious thinking while sparring and when the randomness hits a certain point, bang, your thinking shuts down and you go on automatic. Automatic for any of you may be speeding up, cringing, using only favorite techniques or any one of a hundred things.

You notice that when there are several things going on at once. It becomes hard to concentrate. There are too many distractions. The distraction factor comes from an inability to register several inputs simultaneously in the computer (mind). This is where chaos comes in. You concentrate on one of them and the others still want in. The extra inputs are the random ones, the ones you have not taken control of.

The more attacks thrown quickly at you increases the randomness of that particular exchange.

I have seen instances where a single clash with a high randomness factor will scatter an opponent for several exchanges afterward.

Most people are not trained to handle any kind of randomness or diversity at all. The joke of not being able to walk and chew gum at the same time is a prime example of this.

How does one handle the randomness of an opponent's combinations?

First, slow down to a speed that you can easily handle. Second, work on focusing your attention on what your opponent is doing and catch yourself during attention lapses. Then, slowly increase the speed. Some days are going to feel better than others, so just work on it steadily and it will come.

Do not *try* to do it, just do it. If you try, you are giving yourself room for failure. If you do it, no matter how poorly you do it, you are still doing it. It does not matter how poorly you do something, because just by doing it, you will get better at it.

TIMING

Timing is one of the most important factors in sparring. There is no use in throwing a fast and strong technique if it is not in sync with when your opponent is open for it. Timing is the "when" of sparring. A slower fighter can beat a faster one just by having better timing. Timing involves a decision of when and the certainty of the decision to follow up on it.

There are certain key moments regarding when you should move.

WHEN TO INITIATE OFFENSIVE MOVEMENT ON AN OPPONENT

1. During his stance change, weight shift
2. During his footwork
3. During his hand position change
4. During his advance
5. During his retreat
6. During his reaction to a fake.
7. When he comes to a halt or stand still.

WHEN TO COUNTER

1. As the attacker changes
2. As the ranges cross
3. Before the first attack completes
4. Between attacks
5. As the attacker quits (in range or out)
6. As the attacker retreats

When you begin to work on timing, start slowly. You will start by going through an actual thought process of deciding when. An attack comes in, block, "now!", you counter.

Your opponent switches stance and in mid-step, "now!", you attack. As you get better at timing your attacks and counters, you will begin to shift from thought processes to "picture image recognition." Picture image recognition is when you recognize what is happening and give *an appropriate response for the situation as it is right then.* This happens when you are in tune with what both you and your opponent are doing.

Do not confuse this with a circuit. A circuit will be the same type attack or response for the general same type situation. This is where a circuit will hang you up; there is no such thing as a "general same type situation." Each encounter or clash is a new clash with your opponent, even if it involves the same approach and technique over and over again.

Example: Your opponent throws a back fist and you under punch. Fine. Say you always under punch counter to a back fist. The next time your opponent starts to back fist, you automatically under punch. He checks his back fist and blocks your punch and then follows up by punching you. Had you been in tune with your opponent, you would have seen him check his back fist and then given *an appropriate response* to that particular situation, which may have been checking your punch, changing the target of the punch, or whatever.

You become good as a fighter in direct proportion to your awareness of you, your opponent and your given situation.

The reasons for poor timing are indecision, lack of certainty in a decision made or being out of sync with your opponent.

Indecision

You cannot decide what to do and when to do it. You are in a perpetual fog.

Lack of certainty in a decision made

You do not think the decision you made was right.

Out of sync with your opponent

Your actions do not correspond with what your opponent is doing.

Good cross reference aids for timing are the portions on *circuitry* and *gradient learning.*

TRUST YOUR HUNCHES

Most of what I write and teach is in the realm of the technical and mechanical, but this is one piece I would like to pass on that deals with the intuitive. How many times has it happened that after an exchange you were thinking, "I knew I should have . . . ."

You "knew," but how did you know? Ask an aikidoist and he will say you felt your opponent's ki. Ask Joe Lewis and he will say that your body is reacting to your opponent's aura (I asked him in a seminar, once).

Me? I think you are consciously or unconsciously "reading" your opponent's intention directed at you. Sometimes I just "know" and there have been times I have actually seen a picture image in my mind—a polaroid print in full color.

This is not ruled by principles concerning the physical. It is more in the realm of the intuitive or sixth sense. Do not rule it out. Open your viewpoint up so as to include the possibility of intuitively spotting telegraphed messages, and I think you will be surprised. Do not try to feel or receive—just accept that at anytime you may have a hunch about something. Act on it. Pat yourself on the back when it works out and do not worry about it when it does not.

Let me relate two instances of this.

1. When I fought Fred King for a grand championship match in Vancouver, B.C., Canada, we were in overtime and I got this huge 16″ × 20″ picture image in my mind of him firing a left leg front kick at me. I was immediately ready for it. He started to move and I did an angle step forward and lead jab to the face inside of his . . . yep, front kick, for the match point.

2. Another time, this time in the school, I was feeling particularly good and I noticed that I was looking at, of all places, my opponent's stomach. I felt there was the connection between me and my opponent at that time.

Now, the first instance is an example of reading intention and the second instance could be interpreted as feeling your opponent's ki or feeling your opponent's body aura extending toward you. It does not really matter which explanation is the "officially approved" one. What matters is to open your viewpoint to accept the possibility of it happening and then validate yourself when it does. Do not put it in the realm of the magically mystical or the spoon-bending paranormal—just trust your hunches.

COMMON MISTAKES IN SPARRING

Here are what I consider to be the most common mistakes that are made when sparring. Much of what is listed here, when used as part of a strategic ruse, are not mistakes but assets. But, when you get stuck into any one (or several) of these and it hampers your adaptability in sparring, it is a mistake. Anything that gets in the way of the ability to change will trip you up, and your patterns will be readable, no matter how skilled you are at them. And if you fight out of patterns, you can be set up. So read through these, see which apply and then have somebody else run through them and checklist you also. The most obvious mistakes are ones you are blind to.

1. Too much withdrawal (defense without countering): This will show you are weak on the counter attack and probably have a preference for sneak attacks. Once you get running backwards, it is hard to shift gears and counter attack. Runners generally are not that aggressive.

2. Inefficient footwork in conjunction with hard attacks: You cannot smack your opponent if you cannot get there and you are not going to get there by "stumble footing."

3. Only using your most coordinated side for hitting: This was popularized by Bruce Lee and later by Bill Wallace. I basically disagree with this. I feel it is better in the long run to become well rounded than being a specialist; a specialist is more easily typecast. Besides, so far I have seen only one Bruce Lee and only one Bill Wallace. In their respective approaches to sparring, no one else yet comes close.

4. Not picking targets—random hitting: Do not rely on your backup hits to do the damage for you. A sharp shooter will pick you to pieces.

5. Reaching for blocks: There is a big difference between intercepting and reaching. Intercepting is meeting in mid-flight, and reaching is extending out, chasing down the attack.

6. Standing only one side facing (left or right): Besides having a variety of attacks with both limbs, having a variety of positions you can operate out of is going to typecast you less. Standing with only one side facing is a limiter.

7. Relying on favorite techniques/approaches: Cross reference this with circuits. This is basically circuit thinking.

8. Time lag between block and counter.

9. Time lag between consecutive hits. Both 8. and 9. are of the same idea. Any combination of movements are one action. If you break up the action with pauses, your opponent can hit you during the pause.

10. Trying too hard to win: Trying to win and wanting to win in a contest match are fine, but when you try too hard you will put too much effort into what you are doing, tense up and actually slow down your muscular action and develop tunnel vision that will open you up for counters.

11. Not monitoring your opponent while attacking: Cross reference blind commitment on "Total Commitment" section.

12. Posing after an attack, quitting in range: This comes from too much tournament karate based on the one punch kill idea. If you are in range, do something, anything!

13. Lack of commitment: Halfway measures will produce halfway results.

14. Inappropriate distancing. Being either too close or too far away from your opponent's size and what he is doing.

15. Lack of hips in hitting: This is applicable where rotation power is used. It is easy to fall into hitting just with an independent unit, forgetting to put weight behind your hit.

16. Pulling your blows too short/not being close enough to hit: This is prevalent in schools that do not practice with some sort of contact equipment. This often happens in correlation with #14.

17. Hesitation: This is indecision to do an action or lack of certainty to carry out an action that has been decided upon. Decide and do it.

FINAL NOTES: MY PERSONAL ATTITUDE TOWARD KARATE

Many times I have been asked, "What kind of karate do you teach?" When I answer "American Freestyle," they usually say, "Oh, tournament karate." My "claim to fame" comes from the fact that I am known for being a competitor in tournament karate for a number of years. I was first rated in *Karate Illustrated*'s Top 10 Rating in 1972 and have been in every top karate publication since then, usually in conjunction with tournaments. Tournament karate is my fun karate, but it is not all there is.

As an instructor, I have several conditions I go by when teaching my students: 1) Make it as uncomplicated to learn as possible. 2) Make it as enjoyable as possible. 3) Do not overwhelm a student with too much information in any given class. 4) Teach them what works. My first concern with a new student is to make sure karate is enjoyable and stick to workable basics.

I feel that the first nine months of instruction are going to make or break a potentially good karate player. Here is his infancy, so to speak. This is when he picks up training habits, thinking habits, attitudes pertaining to competition, other types of karate and martial arts in general. The instructor's influence here is stronger than at any other time, so here is where you really have to treat your student right.

Therefore I teach straight karate for about a year before ever attempting to get students to seriously think about tournaments. Until then, it is just a take it or leave it fun thing. After that, I impress upon them its importance in their overall training.

Tournament karate is a training exercise (hopefully a fun one), no more, no less, and should be looked at as such. It is a small piece of the overall pie. To concentrate on only one small aspect and exclude the rest from your viewpoint is damaging to your overall skill and knowledge.

Fluidity, water-tight defense, accurate hitting and technical coordination should be of prime mechanical importance while relaxation, maintaining an easy control and knowing what you are doing is of prime mental importance.

The maintenance of relaxed control under pressure and not giving up when you are losing are of prime importance when entering tournaments. Tournament psyche out is at least 90 percent self-induced. Any time you are nervous or worried about some part of the tourney (your matches, how you will perform, how good your opponent is) *you* are the one who is worrying and therefore *you* are the one blowing your own cool.

Tournaments are often overused as a means of glorification, both for the individual and for the school. Using tournaments for personal gratification is fine until there is an overkill of that idea and you begin to downgrade everyone else. Also, an overkill of the same idea is to attempt to perpetuate a moment of glory gained at a contest. Then, the prime function of the school turns into turning out tournament players who may or may not be prepared for a street fight.

Basically, a karate player should endeavor to be balanced between all points of karate fighting so that he becomes "the calm in the midst of a storm." Fluid, hard, fast, slow, soft, win, lose, attack, block, exercise, etc., he is the central point controlling these approaches and attitudes, and does not allow the attitudes and approaches to control him.